The Story of the Malverns

With Appendices and Illustrations

By

G. W. Hastings

Author of 'A Vindication of Warren Hastings'

British Library Cataloguing-in-Publication Data
A catalogue record for this book is available from the
British Library

CONTENTS

LIST OF ILLUSTRATIONS

MAPS

I. GEOLOGIC MALVERN

THE Malvern Hills run north and south for some twelve miles on the western side of the Severn valley, and form a singularly picturesque object to the eye, not being rounded like most English hills, but presenting a peaked and mountainous outline. Edmund Burke observed this peculiarity, and spoke of them as being the backbone of Gloucestershire. This was a mistake in geography, as nearly the whole of the range is the dividing line between the counties of Worcester and Hereford; but the description nevertheless was apt, for the appearance of the Hills, seen from a distance, somewhat resembles the spinal vertebrae. Byron, when brought as a boy by his mother to Cheltenham, pined for the Highland mountains of his childhood, and used to climb the Cotswolds behind the town to look on the Malverns with tears in his eyes. It was not known to the future poet, nor does it occur to many even in this scientific age, that the peculiar aspect of the Malverns is owing to their volcanic origin. But it is with this fact that their history must begin.

When the late Sir James Dawson, Principal of the M'Gill University at Montreal, delivered at the Birmingham Town Hall, in 1881, his address as President of the British Association, he gave his opinion that the Malvern Hills were undoubtedly the most ancient land in Great Britain, and were probably older than any mountain range in Europe. It may be observed that a day or two before his address Dawson had been on the Hills with the writer, and had shown himself fully cognizant of their geological origin. That origin dates from the Silurian sea which, at a period of remotest antiquity, flowed deep and unbroken over what now is Britain. Its age cannot be known, but looking to the statement by Sir Robert Ball that our planet must have been in existence for 100 millions of years, and to the opinion of Sir Charles Lyell that its geological record is of double that number, it would be difficult to compute the period of that primeval sea at less than many millions of the amount. Let us, in saying this, consider a few only of the many geological events which have succeeded the subsidence of its waves.

Take, for instance, some of the secondary formations. Out of the several Limestone deposits, all produced by the slow action of carbonate of lime on sand and water, all full of marine fossils, shells, corals, star-fishes, crustacea (of which in fact whole mountain ranges are made up), proving the time that must have been required for their deposition, take, let us say, the Carboniferous Limestone. It is the making of this formation which has supplied the world with coal, by depositing layers of vegetable matter, year after year, century after century, age after age, solidifying them by heat and pressure and converting them into fuel. Who can reckon the time required for such slow deposition and such subsequent process over vast areas and at mighty depths? Take again the wide plains of the Permian Sandstone laid down later than the Limestones, the sand all formed from small fragments washed or torn from pre-existing rock, rounded by the action of moving water and deposited, bed by bed, at the bottom of the sea, there to be, by weight and pressure, compacted into rock. These sandstones are frequently found to be many hundreds of feet in depth. Who will count the years that were spent upon their growth? Then again the Lias formation, with its wide diffusion, its multiplicity of new animal forms, reptilian and marsupial, claims another mighty draft upon time for its development and subsequent declension. But more wonderful still is the Chalk, spread over a wide surface, both terrestrial and submerged, all created by the silent, unceasing work of minute organisms, the *foraminifera*, each secreting from sea-water its tiny shell which drops to the bottom as its owner dies, thus laying down in their fleeting but innumerable lives whole continents of the future, as they are doing now in the bed of the Atlantic, and did ages since in the deep, still waters of ancient seas. Look at our chalk cliffs, remember that they are only the rim of the great trench which holds the Channel, of the wide basins in which Paris and London stand, and then, considering their slow growth by the tiniest influences, say whether the mind can number the duration of these awful immensities in the past.

The above is a very brief and imperfect review of some of the secondary rocks, with their chief characteristics. All that have been mentioned were subsequent to the Silurian age. There still remains the Tertiary epoch, with its prolonged history, divided by Sir Charles Lyell into its Eocene, Miocene, and Pleistocene periods, as it approached in its organisms and products, its fauna and flora, to the earth as it appears in its human age. We should tremble did we think of enumerating the changes and transitions, the events and catastrophes which fill, in man's imperfect view, its varied annals. Near to this epoch occurred, over our northern hemisphere, the cataclysm of at least one Ice Age, when the climate grew more and more arctic, until by far the greater part of Britain was covered with an ice-cap like that which now enshrouds Greenland. It may be taken as certain that while the cold was increasing, with glaciers forming on the hills and icebergs floating down from the north-west, there was simultaneously a gradual sinking of the land, probably prolonged till the highest peaks in our island were submerged, and there ensued the covering of its surface with a vast amount of clay and boulders, the deposition of which by floating ice is to be traced to this day in various parts of our country. Then came a change; the land rose again, the climate grew milder, the ice receded, vegetation resumed its sway, and all around favoured the reappearance of animal life in its thousand varieties. Such an oscillation may probably have occurred more than once, but any way this slow process of sinking and rising, this change to arctic climate, and this return to temperate conditions, must have occupied a vastly prolonged period, a period compared with which the subsequent history of man sinks into insignificance. Yet this was only one of the concluding scenes in the mighty drama. Well might the French philosopher exclaim that the work of creation had been carried out with 'the sublime slowness of an Eternal Being'. Yet all the changes which have been thus imperfectly described, this long succession of deposited strata, these countless evolutions of myriads of species, took place subsequent to the movements in that old Silurian sea where the Malvern Hills took their origin. Can there then be any error in dating that origin by many millions of years? Or can any one impugn the opinion of Sir James Dawson that those Hills are the most ancient land in Britain?

That primitive Silurian sea must, conjecturally, have been somewhat shallow, receiving drift of some sort with consequent deposition, and in that deposit were, as usual, the sundry forms of marine life then existent in the locality. We know that volcanic energy was at work in the sea-bed, and by its agency a mass of igneous rock consisting mainly of syenite, but with quartz and some mica intermixed, was protruded, thus forming a submarine reef. There is no trace of any crater, nor is there actual indication of any outpour of lava, though at a low point of the Hills (Wind's Point) there may be some possible appearances of that nature; and it was in that locality that the late Dr. Holl, a scientific observer, correlated the geological conditions with those of the Laurentian rocks of Canada. But on the whole it may be taken as certain that the line of plutonic rock was pushed bodily, by subterranean forces, into the waters of the Silurian sea; that it was gradually, and probably with long periods of quiescence between the repeated movements of upheaval, raised from a submarine reef to the altitude of a marine mountain. It was in this way, and through this incalculable time, that the Malvern Hills took their form and growth.

But then at some indeterminate date during their formation, probably an early date, certainly one within the submarine reef period, a curious event or rather series of events occurred, the discovery of which in our own day has caused the origin of the Malverns to become clear to apprehension. The tale of the wonder must be told as it was brought to light. Rather more than half a century since, it was determined to construct a railway from Worcester to Hereford; the line as laid down by the engineers, wisely or unwisely, was to pass through the Hills a little to the south of Great Malvern, and it thus became necessary to bore a long tunnel. Perhaps the opinion of no geologist had been taken as to the qualities of plutonic rock; perhaps the engineers employed had experience only of tunnelling through sedimentary strata ; but, however that may be, it is certain that the expectations entertained were falsified. Two contractors in succession threw up the work in despair, the adamantine nature of the rock, fired to a crystalline degree by volcanic heat, having defied their efforts. The third was more fortunate. Not long after he commenced operations he found that his workmen had passed into a soft layer, in effect a sedimentary deposit, buried deep in the syenitic substance of the Hills. The spot was examined by geologists, both local and from the British Museum, and its history became clear. In that period of remotest antiquity which we have described there had been a fissure in the submarine reef, and into that fissure there had drifted a loose deposit, with shells and other organisms of Silurian age, which were thus preserved as they were laid down. At some future time a fresh outburst of subterranean energy had caused the mouth of the fissure to be sealed up, and its contents were, for countless ages, imbedded in the solid rock. The lucky contractor, who thus played the part of *tertius gaudens*, finished the tunnel with ease, his fortune made by the accident of some millions of years bygone. But that accident had also written on the Hills for ever the story of their origin, and in the Hastings Museum at Worcester were preserved, under the sedulous care of Sir Charles Hastings, the fossil proofs of their wondrous pedigree.

During the vast ages that elapsed between the time when the Hills first emerged from the water and that close of the Tertiary period which brought the advent of man to the earth, they witnessed upon their flanks great geological changes. At the present time the highest peak of the Malverns is less than 1,500 feet above sea-level, but it may be taken as certain that the wear of incalculable time, the erosion of water, 'storm, earthquake, hurricane and fire', have much reduced their original height. Before they reached 'upper air' the sedimentary Silurian strata had been laid deep and high on their western side, and above these had come subsequently the Old Red Sandstone formation, occupying in the main the wide expanse of Herefordshire. On the east came at a much later date the New Red Sandstone, which still covers the valley of the Severn with its saliferous strata, lying pretty level at the foot of the Malverns, and thus differentiating the scenery of Worcestershire from that on the Herefordshire side. For whereas the Silurian formations, running high on the western slope of the Hills, dwarf their height and give them that aspect of a wooded eminence so common in English scenery, the comparative flatness of the Sandstone on the east leaves the Hills free to rise in mountain picturesqueness, presenting a view rare enough in the more southern portion of our island. But this was not always so. Excavation for building purposes in the town of Malvern has shown that the Sandstone formerly rose some 600 feet above sea-level, and rested slantingly upon the plutonic rock. No trace of dislocation or disturbance has been discovered ; the deposit seems to have been laid down placidly at a time when one-half at least of the present height must have been under water. In truth there must have been a great denudation on the eastern flank of the Malverns, and that too in some of the later stages of geological history. It may be well to give a reason for this opinion. Sir Roderick Murchison believed that the whole extent of country between the Malverns and the Cotswolds was once a sea flowing from what is now the mouth of the Dee to what is now the exit of the Severn into the Bristol Channel, thus making Wales, with the part of England west of the Malverns, into an island. To this sea he gave the name of the Straits of Malvern, an expanse of water which, as the land rose in the later Tertiary period, subsided into a broad tidal estuary, and finally into the three river streams of the Severn, the Avon, and the Teme. Into these Straits would pour the bergs which came down from the north-west up to the close of the Ice Age. When the writer saw the Straits of Belle Isle, separating the coast of Labrador from the Island of Newfoundland, he was struck with the similarity which they bear to the Straits of Malvern as conceived by the geological mind of Murchison. He (the writer) received at Montreal from the hands of Sir James Dawson a report made by Lieutenant Vaughan, R.N., then custodian of the lighthouse on Belle Isle, describing his experience for the twelve months then past. He stated that during that time no less than 800 large bergs had passed the entrance to the Straits, making their way to the south-west. It may be interesting to record, as showing the extent of that ice action which is one of the most suggestive incidents of geological inquiry, that in his opinion the number of bergs which passed to the east of Newfoundland was more than double those which entered the Straits. Now supposing that the icebergs floating down every year from the glaciers of the north-west in the late Tertiary times were no more than those which crash and scrape through the narrow sea at Belle

Isle, what must have happened to the surface layers in the Straits of Malvern? Is it not certain that they were so ploughed and scraped by the great bergs grinding their way by sheer weight over all obstacles, and bearing before them the lighter material, that every year more or less, and usually the more rather than the less, those layers were borne away down the current of the Straits? In this way the upper portion of the New Red Sandstone was inevitably carried off, the sides of the Hills on the east being flayed as it were of their covering, and left bare down to, or nearly to, the level of the then sinking sea. Much the same, it may be conjectured, happened at a like period to the Lias, which remains in a broad belt of country on the eastern border of what was once the Severn estuary, but has wholly disappeared from the lower level of the Severn valley. It may be that the current which brought down the bergs into the Straits, and which must have flowed strongly round the projection made by the Clees, would not have affected the eastern so much as the western and middle waters, where the dredging work of the bergs was done, and thus it was that the Lias was preserved on the one side of Worcestershire while it was swept off on the other. This is of course a hypothetical, but it is submitted a not improbable solution of a question which has attracted locally the notice of geologists.

At all events the Straits of Malvern, as they gradually passed away through the uprising of the land, left the Hills, so far as their natural aspect and surroundings were concerned, much as they are at present. There was the wonderful breadth of prospect and diversity of view, save that these were then unscarred by any works of man, being in one part shrouded by dark forest, and silvered in another by the wide tidal stream. But above all the Hills remained the relics and the witness of a mighty past. They had emerged from the waters when all was unbroken sea around them. They had lasted through the growth and decay of formation after formation. Before the Alps were they had been. Countless living organisms had come and gone, type after type had been called into being and had passed away. They had subsided in the waves and had again risen from the deep. None can tell their generations, for everything about the Malverns, in their natural aspect, bears the stamp of an almost incredible antiquity. To many, no doubt, it seems a strange thought. For millions of years the earth rolled in its course, suns rose and set, nature maintained her order, life existed in endless variety, all without man's presence, untouched by his genius, and undisturbed by his inquietude. Some may say, what then was the use? What conscious intelligence was there? What voice of worship, what sign of recognition, rose to the Maker of all? Perhaps there is more faith, as well as more poetry, in the utterance of Milton :—

> nor think, though men were none,
> That heaven would want spectators, God want praise.
> Millions of spiritual creatures walk the earth,
> Unseen, both when we wake and when we sleep.
> All these with ceaseless praise His works behold,
> Both day and night.[1]

But there is a fuller answer to these blind questions. Man came. His advent was the crown and explanation of the long drama. His diviner form, through countless generations of life, had grown out of the lower shapes. Comparative anatomy attests his relationship to them, and confirms his dominion over them. The completed design vindicates the eternal Craftsman. In this, as in so many things, Natural Science is handmaid in the temple of God.

Yet the ancient man who stood upon the Malvern heights, long centuries before human history began, might well have regarded himself as primitive, though in truth, geologi-

[1] *Paradise Lost*, Book iv.

cally speaking, he was utterly modern. Archaic specimens of humanity have been discovered on the continent, and it might be difficult even to conjecture their antiquity, but the earliest human inhabitants of our island, so far as our present knowledge extends (except perhaps in one doubtful case), were the cave-dwellers whose relics have been found in various localities. Their period was of course ancient, but it does not appear to date further back than the time when the Ice Age was slowly passing away from Europe.

It is these cave-dwellers, or their immediate successors, who may now claim our consideration.

II. PREHISTORIC MALVERN

There is no actual trace of cave-dwellers on the Malverns, though the circumstances of the locality would in some respects have been favourable to such a settlement. All the caves which can be proved to have been inhabited by early races are situated very near to seas, lakes, or rivers. The convenience for fishing was the obvious cause. In this case the broad waters of the Severn estuary would have supplied the want. But the solid igneous rock of the Hills would not permit caverns, and the Red Sandstone deposit below would at that remote period have probably been covered by the tidal stream. It may, however, be noted that not far from the Malverns there was once a settlement of cave-dwellers, of which it may be permitted to give some description. On the banks of the Wye, an ultimate tributary of the Severn, situated between Symond's Yat and Chepstow, high in the cliffs of the left bank, is a line of caverns which were inhabited by prehistoric man. Several of them have been examined, and contain proofs of human occupation, probably at different periods. There are floors of stalagmite which could only have been formed by the slow process of dripping from the rock above, involving a long period of time, and beneath these floors were found bones of the animals which had afforded food for the cave-dwellers and stone weapons fashioned from the flint for use. But a still more convincing proof of remote antiquity is found in the position of the caverns. It is certain that when used by the ancient inhabitants they must have been near to the river. At the present time they are at least two hundred feet above it. The river-bed has been lowered by the ceaseless erosion of water. What period of time was required to effect this excavation it would be difficult to say, but we know that the retrocession of the falls on the Niagara river over not many miles has been calculated at many thousands of years, and we may be sure that the cutting away of the cliffs from Chepstow to a point far beyond these caverns must have lasted for untold centuries. We have here one of the many proofs of the vast antiquity of man. It has long been known that the date of earthenware vessels found deep in the alluvial soil of Egypt cannot be reckoned at less than 20,000 years, and if that be the age of a civilization, rude it may be but of social community capable of manufacture, what are we to allow to the primitive cave-dwellers, living in precarious conflict with the beasts of the field? Yet they must have looked on Britain much as it is now, in respect to its broad natural features, though its climate, during their prolonged occupation, may have varied more than once from extremer cold to more torrid heat than is ever experienced now.

But there was a race more capable coming on, more capable in reality, though we may look back on them now with pity or disdain, as half-civilized. We know nothing of the genesis of any new race; its beginnings are always shrouded in the mystery amid which Nature works. There can be no reason to believe that the Lapps sprang from the cave-dwellers; and except as to their probable origin in Asia, we are ignorant alike whence they came and from whom they were descended. They were not the earliest race known in Britain, but they were the first which survived the many chances of destruction awaiting a primitive people. At whatever date they arrived here, they had already spread over a great part of the Continent. Their relics show that they were as numerous in the valley of the Seine as they were in that of the Thames, that they hunted the reindeer in the south of France, and were existent on the slopes of the Pyrenees.

They appeared before history began, and they are in evidence and prolific still. Others have died out, but they have lived on, and will last yet. That fact alone stamps them as a race not to be despised, for it proves that they possess vitality. What makes them more interesting is that they have not changed in any important particular their mode of life, habits, or perhaps any of their characteristics, since they were in Britain in prehistoric times. They were then no doubt, as they are now, a simple, quiet, pastoral race, small in stature, with little invention or enterprise, rudimentary morality and much content. It is easy to imagine them encamped in rude huts on the eastern flank of the Malverns, their reindeer cropping the short grass of the Hills and the coarser herbage of the scanty soil below, and themselves fishing in the tidal waters of what was still an estuary, or in winter snaring fish in ice-holes. Here, as elsewhere over a wide area in the slowly improving climate of Europe, they lived in quiet till a much greater race, advancing from the east and south, drove them from their haunts, drove them perpetually to the west and north, helpless and unresisting, till they finally found their rest within the Arctic circle on both sides of the Pole. Probably they clung longer to Ireland than they did to

Britain. Sir Harry Johnston seems to think that he observed a trace of them on the west coast of Connaught. It is also quite likely that they left some legacies of their habits and superstitions among the far superior race before whom they disappeared. That may be taken as the usual consequence when a population, however sparse and feeble, is gradually dispossessed by an invader.

The invaders in this case were the Iberians, a Turanian race from that nursery-ground of European nations, the central plateau of Asia ; somewhat short in stature, but sturdy in make, apt for war and enterprise, and gifted with brains which could both invent and execute. Before this energetic people the primitive Lapps must have melted like snow in the sun. They spread over all England and have left, unless archaeologists are altogether mistaken, abiding proofs of their genius. Many of the hill fortresses and other earthworks which were formerly attributed to the Kelts are now believed to have been the work of the Iberians. A number of our popular superstitions, ancient customs, and rural habits are credited to this people, though it may be, as already hinted, that they in their conquest had assimilated some Lapp peculiarities. With respect to hill fortresses, there are some remarkable entrenchments on the southern heights of the Malverns which must have required stupendous labour to execute, and have been designed to serve some permanent and important object. These works command the pass which has always existed between the east and the west on each side of the Hills, and ultimately between South Wales and central England. The common opinion has been that they were the work of the Kelts, or as they are usually termed the ancient Britons. It is probable enough that during the great struggle between Caractacus and the Roman legions under Ostorius this hill fortress was occupied by the Britons. It must have been impregnable on the eastern side, and they may have thought, not knowing the resources of Roman strategy, that it was little likely to be assailed on the western. But there has always been, among the students of the subject, a floating idea that Ostorius, after his decisive victory, probably won near the upper waters of the Teme, marched by the west flank of the Malverns, took the entrenchments above the Wind's Point on their weaker side (weaker because situated on the high slope of the Silurian deposits), and either stormed the camp, or starved its occupants into surrender. All this may possibly be true, but it does not prove that the Kelts had constructed the camp, any more than the name of the Herefordshire village below, Colwall, no doubt *Collis Vallum,* and the finding of Roman coins thereabouts, prove that, contrary to all Roman usage, it was made by the legions. One thing is certain, that by whomsoever it was constructed, and to whatever purpose it was at any time applied, it was originally beyond question a prehistoric work.

These entrenchments run round the whole surface of the hill, they are in a double line, and are surmounted by a third ditch enclosing what was obviously meant to be the citadel, where the last desperate resistance was to be made. There was room within the outer circuit for a considerable number of fighting men, probably for a whole tribe, possibly for women and children and even cattle also. Outside, a little to the south-west, is a supply of water from a natural spring, which still flows down the hill. The whole work was admirably engineered, and must for its completion have required huge labour. To whom are we to attribute the conception and execution of this great prehistoric monument? There will always be a difference of opinion on the point, but we incline to the belief that it is a relic of Iberian genius and of Iberian steadfastness in work. There is on the Hills, not far beyond it, another and much smaller camp, showing some of the peculiarities observed in Keltic fortification, especially the entrance fitted for chariots, which were a Keltic institution, and the turn in the opening skilfully contrived to compel the invading charioteer to expose his unshielded side to the enemy. The merit of this second encampment may be conceded to the ancient Britons. Both are clearly prehistoric; but the palm in the way of greatness must be given to the Iberians.

Much the same may be said on another topic. For generations it was implicitly believed that Stonehenge was Keltic. Possibly it was so; but there is much to be said on the other side, and the whole subject is now better understood than it was formerly. Sir Norman Lockyer and other astronomers have been at the pains to investigate the age of Stonehenge in connexion with the precession of the equinoxes, and the result has been brought out clearly. It seems that Stonehenge was built certainly as early as 1500 B.C., probably as early as 1750, and quite possibly as far back as 2000. This has been ascertained by first marking the position of the sun, in relation to the eastern entrance of Stonehenge, at its rising in the summer solstice; and then on the assumption, which may safely be made, that the temple was so built that the sun's rays should shine through that entrance on the solstice morning, calculating the period necessary for the change at the present day of the sun's position in the heavens. Taking the calculation as correct, some serious questions arise as to the builders of Stonehenge. If the Kelts built it at the latest date given, 1500 B. C., they must have been in Britain at a considerably earlier date, and that for two reasons. First, while it is not disputed that they vanquished and drove out the Iberians, it is certain that the conquest of such a sturdy race was not effected in a day. Their success is usually attributed to two factors; the one that they were a taller people with longer arms, which would give them a great advantage in the days of personal combat; the other that they knew the use of iron for their weapons, whereas the Iberians had only bronze. Nevertheless the work of subjugation must have been slow, especially if the Iberians, as is believed to have been the case, were masters of castrametation. Secondly, it would seem that Stonehenge is probably the climax of the art which erected its grand proportions, and a long period must be allowed for that art's rise and development. There are other stone circles in the country, built apparently for the same sun-worship, but far inferior in design and construction. To take one example; the circle of the Rollright Stones, some four miles from Chipping Norton in Oxfordshire, was undoubtedly a sun-temple. At the east end of the circle one of the stones has an orifice, made artificially as the marks within it testify, through which the rays of the rising sun could at the solstice penetrate the circle. No one could think of comparing the Rollright Stones with Stonehenge; the stones are much smaller and the construction much more rude; but the design for worship was the same; and the race which made the one in all reasonable probability made the other. Probably the Rollright circle is from 500 to 1,000 years more ancient than Stonehenge, and if Kelts were the builders, and the foregoing calculations be correct, it would follow that they had been in Britain for a period of from 3,000 to 4,000 years when Julius Caesar invaded our island. We hesitate to accept such a conclusion; we should be inclined to conjecture that the years of Keltic occupation could not at that time have been more than half the number.

Moreover let us consider the account of Keltic religion given in his Commentaries by Caesar. His statement of the manners and customs of the ancient Britons was obviously founded on information which he believed to be trustworthy, and was probably obtained in conversation with the chiefs who met him to negotiate a peace. He tells us that the Britons worshipped several deities, whom he named by their Latin appellations, and among them is Apollo. But he does not name Apollo first, nor assign to him any superiority over the others, nor does he give any hint that the sun was the prime, much more the sole object of worship. Moreover he says that their cult was carried on in the depths of forests, among sacred trees, and nowhere does he say a word about any temple. It would be difficult to connect this account with the circular stone temples, situated on open hills or wide moors, and dedicated, as their structure and surroundings show, to the appearance of the sun at the solstice. Nor is it possible to ignore the negative evidence implied by the absence in Caesar's narrative of any mention of Stonehenge. That structure was so vast and remarkable that if it had been a place where the Britons were accustomed to worship it must have been the most noted as such in the land, and would surely have been named to him when he was inquiring of those in authority concerning their religion. The only conclusion we can arrive at is that Stonehenge was neither used nor venerated by the Keltic Britons, that it had not been built by them, and consequently must have been built by a preceding race, which race could only be the Iberian.

That conclusion arrived at, we are able to form some estimate of the people. They must have been at once gifted and powerful, possessed at an early period of arts and knowledge which we are accustomed to associate with considerable civilization. The construction of Stonehenge, for instance, must have required not only much manual skill, but a trained acquaintance with the use of the lever and the pulley, and an aptness for organizing labour. The great monoliths which to this day excite the wonder of beholders had to be brought from a distance no nearer than the Mendips, in the face of difficulties which can now only be conjectured; were raised to their destined positions by an art requiring a practised eye and nice calculation, and arranged in a sacred order inspired no less by astronomical observation than by religious fervour. There can be no reason for entering into disquisitions as to the extent or depth of knowledge of the heavenly bodies possessed by this people. It is enough to know that they could calculate the return of the solstices, and probably used the rising of certain stars as guides for their observations. That is interesting enough without inquiring into the how and why of their knowledge or speculating on any connexion with the building of the Egyptian pyramids.

The subjugation of such a race must have taken a long period, and it must not be supposed that, even after defeat, the Iberians disappeared as the Lapps had done. Whether by capture or by treaty, whether as slaves or allies, they remained a vigorous and highly intelligent element in the population of the country, largely transmitting their habits and ideas, and in some degree their language, to the mixed race that thence arose in Britain. Their sun-worship had probably come with them from the wide plains of central Asia, where that worship is a natural cult; it must have been rooted in their being, and may have been continued in some of their temples after the conquest. Some writers, indeed, have conjectured that the Druids were really Iberians, but on this point there is an absence of any proof. One thing is certain, that a number of the circles constructed by them are to be seen to this day, and prove their kind of worship.

The Rollright Stones, in North Oxfordshire, have been named already, and may deserve some further notice. They are arranged, some seventy in number, in an exact circle, on the top of the low limestone ridge which marks the boundary between the counties of Oxford and Warwick, and must, when the country was open, have been well placed to catch the earliest rays of the rising sun. The aspect of them has been much damaged by a clump of trees which has been planted in their midst, and it is probable that the roots of these trees have been answerable for the fall of several of the stones. Now that the circle is under the protection of the Crown as a national monument some attention might be given to this matter. The loftiest of the stones still remains erect, and its height, after (say) 4,000 years of wear and tear from weather, is still at least seven feet. Not far from the circle is an outstanding solitary monolith, on a rising ground, concerning which Sir Norman Lockyer conjectures that it may have been designed to mark the rising of some prominent star. A cromlech in the field adjoining the circle has been damaged by a tree planted within the enclosure. It may be observed that all these stones are of the oolitic limestone of the neighbourhood. We think and speak of their antiquity ; but what are their years compared with the measureless periods which produced the material from which they were quarried?

In dealing with this prehistoric age it may

be proper to note that, scattered through Britain, there are a number of ancient ways, hardly to be called roads in our sense of the word, which unquestionably date before history. Such for instance is a way, chiefly on hillsides, which runs from the neighbourhood of Southampton to near Canterbury, and which obtained the name of the Pilgrims' Way, because it was so much used by visitants to the shrine of Thomas à Becket. But few antiquarians can doubt that it was prehistoric, to whatever race it may owe its origin. Now there is one of these old grass-grown, mysterious ways running at the foot of the southern Malverns, starting near to Little Malvern Church and ending at or near to Newent on the Bristol Channel. It runs as straight and it remains as plainly distinguishable as if it had been made yesterday. Was it the Kelts, or was it the Iberians, who used it for communication with the sea? We know not, but it at least bears witness that in days very far bygone there were, below those Hills, human settlements bent on travel and intercourse, communities which have long faded from the minds of men.

We may have seemed, in the preceding pages, to have sometimes gone far from the Malverns, but we have done so for the sake of light and explanation. And, after all, the caves of the Wye are not far from our Hills, the Circle of Rollright is within easy distance of a view across the Severn Valley, and there is an eminence in the Forest of Dean, exhibiting the relics of sun-worship, which commands a prospect of the western flank of the Malverns. All the three races of which we have spoken, Lapp, Iberian, and Kelt, have lived, warred and worshipped beside and upon those immemorial Hills; they all dwelt under the shadow of 'the most ancient land in Britain'.

III. EARLY MALVERN

THE word Malvern, or to use its original form, Mol-vern, signified according to one interpretation the wooded hill, and according to another the bald hill. Probably both were correct in their way, and are reconcile-able. On the one hand it is difficult to understand how the eastern flank of the Hills could ever have been wooded to any height, for it is only in a few parts that, even now, the solid igneous rock will permit an accumulation of soil sufficient to support tree life. On the other hand it seems certain that at the time of the Conquest the whole of the lower slope of the Hills (on the sand-stone) was thickly wooded. So that looking at the height it was bald, looking below it was covered. Moreover, on the western flank, thanks to the Silurian slope, wood no doubt was in older days, as it is now, plenti-ful. The Hills, therefore, may have seemed bald on one side and clothed with trees on the other. But anyway, at the time of which we are speaking, that shortly succeeding the Conquest, the aspect of the Malvern Hills on the Worcestershire side must have been ex-tremely desolate. For some distance below

VIEW OF MALVERN HILLS FROM THE WEST

them the soil was scanty and barren, swept bare as we have ventured to suggest by the icebergs in the glacial and post-glacial periods. To this day it has largely retained that character, and wide spaces still remain which have never been subject to any cultivation beyond that of keeping some sheep. How completely the Hills were given over to this form of produce, and how segregated they were from the country around, may be learned from the fact that there was of old a distinct breed of sheep on the Malverns, resembling the Welsh breed in their small size and, it is believed, in the delicate flavour of their flesh, but nevertheless quite recognizable from them. This breed was still existent in the earlier part of the last century, it was seen and is remembered by the writer, and it lasted, like some other things, while the charm of Malvern as a delightful yet secluded watering-place was still unimpaired. But as population grew and taste died out, the breed was destroyed, as many another variety has been, through contact with the ordinary flocks, to meet the greed of producers. Its early existence must have brought to the spot a certain number of shepherds, and the small immemorial paths that are found on the Hills bear evidence likely enough to their care and watchfulness. Over the width of the waste land below wandered herds of swine, half-wild, accustomed to feed themselves, and yearly gathered in at one particular hill for the purpose of being marked by their owners. This hill, near Malvern Wells, has long been known as the Swinnerd, simply a corruption of the Swine Yard, being a spot where the configuration of the hillside made the collection of the herds convenient. It is easily recognizable still by intelligent observation. The swine again must have necessitated a certain number of guardians and supervisors, and thus have tended to encourage another small population. Lastly, there must from the first have been red deer wandering over Malvern Chase. We are at this moment of our history far from the time of Gilbert de Clare, the Red Earl of Gloucester, who did so much to foster the number of the deer, and laid down forest laws to protect the herds and to punish marauders. But the wild deer were always denizens of the Chase, always the objects of sport, and must have maintained, in one way or another, a certain number of rural settlers. The Hills could not have been altogether without scattered occupants or visitants, neither could the flat below have been wholly untenanted. But it is certain that the country was in the main destitute of population. If it could be described by Bishop Latimer in the sixteenth century as a wild and desolate region, what must it have been in the eleventh? If the good bishop thought that in his time the shelter and hospitality of the Benedictine monastery were necessary for travellers through the Malvern waste, what must have been the need, and what too the dread of any wayfarer three centuries before, who had to cross those Hills without the glimpse of any hostel to cheer his path. Yet the prospect from a little distance, say from the ridge of Powyke, must in those days have been grand. The wide expanse of open land beneath the Hills, the wild peaks rising above, and the look of unapproachable solitude hanging over all, must have produced a striking effect.

In the midst of the hill named the Worcestershire Beacon, the loftiest and finest of the whole range, is a ravine or gully, now partly obliterated, which in old times descended in its entirety to the flat at the bottom. It is quite probable that in prehistoric days this opening was filled with a small glacier, and it has been conjectured that some traces of a moraine were to be found not more than a generation ago. At the head of this gully, about 800 feet above the level of the sea, a stream of water has always gushed out of the rock and made its way to the plain below. The water is exceptionally clear, and flowing as it does from igneous rock, is absolutely free from any organic taint. It was from this stream that Malvern, as an inhabited place, took its rise.

It was in the reign of Henry the First, at the latest, that a certain priest, given to the ascetic side of religion, and caring little for exposure and hardship, found his way to this rivulet, followed its course up the steep side of the ravine till he reached a spot about half-way to its issue from the rock, and resolved to fix his simple dwelling by its waters. That spot, where or whereabouts stood long afterwards a small house called Banister's Cottage, and named in an old map in the custody of the steward of the manor as the Hermitage, marks the then lonely place amid the wilds where the hermit Aldwin served God according to his faith. When, some eighty years since, Banister's Cottage changed hands, and an Italian villa was built beside it, the level of the entrance road or path was altered and the spade disclosed a small number of rough unhewn stones of the hill rock, which were conjectured, and perhaps not without reason, to have been the remains of Aldwin's rude habitation. Such at least was the account given to the writer by an eye-witness.

It must have been a position of utter solitude, some 700 feet above sea-level, far from human intercourse. But in those respects it simply provided the conditions which Aldwin must have sought, and it certainly furnished him with exhilarating air and pure water. What he did for food is unknown, but he may have had a goat, which would have thrived on the short grass of the hill, to supply him with milk. Dr. Kitto, an Eastern traveller, in his *Illustrations of the Bible*, deals with the supply to Elijah at the brook Cherith. His knowledge both of the Hebrew language and of Jewish ways induces him to dismiss the ravens from the story. He points out that the raven was an unclean bird, and therefore an unacceptable agent for supplying food to the prophet. Moreover the word translated as raven has no less than twelve different meanings in the original Hebrew, which can only be differentiated by the 'points', and 'points' were not in use till long after the narrative of Elijah must have been written. Kitto therefore, after due discussion, pronounces in favour of 'Arab', which is one of the twelve meanings, and tells us that the true rendering of the passage would be, 'the Arabs brought him bread and meat in the morning, and bread and meat in the evening; and he drank of the brook.' Nor, as there always have been Bedouin tribes about the borders of Palestine, does there seem anything unreasonable in the conjecture. But this by the way. There were neither Arabs nor ravens to feed Aldwin, but there are helpers under Providence everywhere, and even in that wild region, populated mainly by beasts of the field, deer, swine, sheep, the hermit may well have found some sympathy and have received from time to time some simple aid for his sustenance. He probably afforded spiritual ministrations to the families of the shepherds and swineherds and other peasants who haunted the Hills and the Chase, and their gratitude in some humble ways repaid him. Among the sex which always leans to the side of compassion he would be sure to find friends. Moreover it is certain from all traditional accounts that soon after his life of solitude and abstinence began the fame of it spread over the surrounding country. Numbers came to see the wonderful hermit who abode on Malvern Hill; many of them would bring some offering of their regard, and from that time all difficulty as to his subsistence must have vanished. There is no doubt that he lived and died in a reputation befitting his sanctity, and he has been honoured by remote generations as the founder of Malvern.

But the fame of Aldwin spread far beyond

the shadows of the Hills. It was the age of conventual development, and not only were the pious founders of the day busy in establishing new monasteries for the welfare of their souls, but the older and greater houses aimed at the extension of their influence by creating subsidiary communities. The great order of St. Benedict, whose fame was in all lands, had been planted at Westminster by the Confessor and had been royally endowed by his bounty. The Chapter of the abbey had heard of Aldwin, probably from the Benedictines of Worcester Cathedral or from some other Worcestershire community of their Order. It was obviously an occasion when some recognition was desirable, and it was resolved that a Benedictine monastery should be founded at Malvern as a cell to Westminster. The enterprise was carried out; Aldwin was nominated as the first Prior, and tradition tells that some other hermits who had joined him were associated in the foundation; but further details are unknown; any records that might have thrown light on the inception of the Priory probably perished at the Dissolution. It is, however, reasonable to conjecture that the new community received most of its first members from Westminster, though some perhaps from other houses of the Order in the neighbourhood, near or far, of Malvern. But in all events it was a Westminster foundation, and ever recognized as such by the parent house. The site of the Priory was well chosen. It was high above the valley and yet below the hard rock of the Hills, with the advantage of having its foundation on the relatively soft sandstone. There was a plentiful supply of water, for the stream that issues far above from the virgin rock, the stream that had solaced the hermitage, flowed down from the gully near to the site. Moreover the sandstone beneath the Hills always holds a store of water filtered from the rock, which responds to slight effort in digging. The buildings faced the east, and were by the configuration of the ground partially sheltered from the north. There was a favourable aspect to the south, and the soil sloping down from the Priory to the Chase was tolerably fertile. The community, when once housed, had a promising start, though the surroundings were to a great degree solitary.

Of the original church built by the founders of the Priory only the nave remains, or speaking more strictly only the arches of the nave,[1] which are Norman of an early and somewhat rude type. The whole church indeed was Norman in its architecture, with

[1] To these should perhaps be added the south door, which must have opened into the cloisters.

a flat and no doubt somewhat low roof, and small clerestory windows after the fashion of that period. The length of the church extended as far as to what is now the entrance to the chancel, and there it terminated in an apse. It was a solid building made out of the enduring rock of the Hills, but was an unpretentious structure compared to its successor, to which it had to give way in the much wealthier and much more artistic fifteenth century. But to the few and ignorant inhabitants of the district, unacquainted with any walls but those of their own squalid cottages, the church which now rose beneath the lonely hills must have been an object of wonder and veneration. The services of the monks, with their ordered chanting, must have been something unheard, perhaps undreamed of before. The charity of the religious, always freely—indeed too freely—bestowed, must have attracted not a few; while the cultivation of the conventual fields, necessitating a certain number of hands to help, gave more legitimate increase to the population around. There can hardly be a doubt that the foundation of the Priory created for the first time a Malvern village, and probably a Malvern parish, which latter extended as far as the Severn, embracing the wild space of the Chase on its northern end, and running up the untenanted Hills in empty claim above. Two things more may be noted as works of the monks. They supplied the parish with a humble church and churchyard to the north of their own buildings, and they dedicated the spring of pure water which issued from the rock at the head of the gully we have described to the sanctity of St. Anne, the mother of our Lady. Hence it became a holy well in the estimation of the surrounding country. But there is no trace of any chapel in the church dedicated to St. Anne, the only female saint thus honoured having been St. Ursula.

The community at Malvern was Benedictine. and was therefore learned. It has been said that monasticism was the ark in which classical culture floated down the great flood of the Middle Ages. It would be perhaps more correct to say that the Order of St. Benedict was the ark in question, for undoubtedly there were many monasteries where learning was scant enough. But in the Benedictine libraries Latin literature and Latin philosophy were always present, and usually the monks had a school and handed on their attainments to others. We have in an inscription which has survived the trials of time (it was dug up near the shrine of St. Ursula) a proof that knowledge was cultivated during the early days of Malvern Priory. It is an epitaph on Walcher, the second Prior of the community, and commemorates his attainments, recording that among other things he was 'astrologus'. That does not necessarily mean that he practised what is called astrology, though it is not unlikely that he did so, for in the early days of science a good deal of fanciful superstition, especially as to forecasting the future, was mixed up with a knowledge of the natural world.[1] What the word does mean is that the monk thus distinguished by exceptional gifts among his fellows, was one who watched the heavens, knew the movements of the planets, and made astronomical observations. He must have had a fine opportunity for doing so to the south of the Priory, where in the open waste he would have found nightly an ample exposure of sky. Nor need it be supposed that in the absence of artificial aids to sight he must needs lack the capacity to see and understand. The Greek Thales had no such aids, yet he is believed by many to have antedated the modern knowledge of the solar system. Copernicus, in the cloister of his

[1] 'Astrology and Astronomy were in fact closely identified in the ancient world, and relics of the superstition still linger in Zadkiel almanacs.' *Human Origins.* By S. Laing, p. 143.

monastery at Thorne, had nothing but his naked eye to help him, but his calculations nevertheless upset the conclusions of many centuries, and made a new astronomy for Europe. Galileo began without glasses, and laid down great principles before he used their help, though it was only when his telescope showed him the satellites of Jupiter that his perception of those tiny specks in the heavens finally sealed the doom of the Ptolemean philosophy. That solitary and forgotten observer on the south side of Malvern Priory may well have seen and known more than we may imagine to-day, for as there were brave men before Agamemnon so there were men with deep thoughts and strong brains who saw and calculated and worked out startling conclusions before either Copernicus or Galileo had gazed on the stars. There are unknown forerunners of every discovery, and one of them may have been Walcher who studied his problems under the Malverns. But we may be sure that, if the most erudite, he was not the only philosopher there. On the contrary, it may be taken as certain that the Benedictine monks of Malvern were, from the first, a body learned and inquiring, versed in literature, and by no means wanting in physical science. Their advent on the scene is the point we have now reached.

Let us look for a moment at the long sequence of events through which we have brought the story of the Malvern Hills. We knew them at first as a submarine reef in a sea of fathomless antiquity. We have seen them emerging from the deep to witness the astonishing changes and developments of geological ages, the work of evolution in fish, reptile, bird, and beast, till the world beheld man in the rude cave-dweller. We have been with them as they looked down on a succession of races, Lapp, Iberian, and Kelt, each of which lived its life on our island, fulfilled its destiny and gave way to another. And now we see them sheltering under their cliffs a population of superior breed, scanty in number it may be, but with the blessed presence of Religion and Learning, twin sisters assuring them of light in their present darkness and providing in the future for their protection and peace.

IV. MEDIEVAL MALVERN

In the thirteenth century Gilbert de Clare, commonly called on account of the colour of his hair the Red Earl of Gloucester, was a mighty hunter before the Lord. To him, on his marriage with Joan d'Acres, the daughter of the king, Edward the First had granted Malvern Chase, a tract of country on the east flank of the Hills, reputed to be twenty miles in length north and south, with its herds of red deer and all its forest powers, manorial rights and privileges. An old writer, Leland, says concerning it: 'The Chase of Malvern is bigger than either Wyre or Feckenham, and occupies a great part of Malvern Hills. Great Malvern and Little also is set in the Chase. The highest point is about 1,313 feet above the surface of the Severn at Hanley.' It was at Hanley that the Earl built his castle, where he and his successors lived and ruled in the midst of the Chase. The Conquerer is said by another old writer to have loved those red deer as if they had been his children; he desolated whole districts, expelling the inhabitants to make room for them, and he enacted forest laws of cruel severity to protect the herds from molestation. The New Forest remains to this day an abiding witness to his love of the deer.

Gilbert de Clare was a worthy imitator of the great Norman. Under his rule Malvern Chase was kept strictly afforested, and many miles of country which have now for two centuries and a half been open to cultivation and increase, were then practically shut out from mankind and devoted mainly to beasts of the chase. His territory ran to the top of the Hills, where it met the border of another county, and provoked a collision with another authority. In those days, go where you would, you came across episcopal property and claims, and the rival with whom De Clare had in this instance to deal was the bishop of Hereford. A fierce dispute arose between them. Clerics, as much as laymen, were fond of sport, and were as little disposed to tolerate interference with their claims. Such of the annals of the abbey of St. Albans as have come to light, annals of which, for some reason, the ecclesiastical writers of the day seem to fight somewhat shy, show that the abbots were continually engaged in disputes with neighbours brought on by their game-preserving. There can be no reason to suppose that they differed from many other abbots. Nor did the bishop of Hereford, in all probability, differ much from many other bishops. He loved hunting, and he liked venison, and naturally so did they. It appears that the quarrel between the earl and the ecclesiastic was of some duration, but it was finally terminated by a work which has to this day left its mark on the Malvern Hills. A deep ditch was dug under the direction of De Clare along the ridge of the Hills from the Worcestershire Beacon to the southern end where they run into Gloucestershire. At the Wind's Point it joined the outer line of the great entrenchments that had been made there untold centuries before, but the construction of the road across the Hills has obliterated the ditch in that quarter. It was a great undertaking, characteristically Norman in its boldness and completeness, and when it had been achieved the Red Earl published his edict that any Herefordshire man found on the eastern side of the trench should lose his right hand. Such was his way of dealing with poachers. There is no doubt that his forest rule was strict and that in his day the red deer were multiplied, but it may also be remembered that this same period in English history witnessed the first summons by the Crown of that Commons'

House which was destined from generation to generation to curb the oppressions under which the people suffered.

In the meantime the Priory grew and flourished. Henry the First had approved its foundation, had endowed it with, among other lands, Quat and Fulford in Staffordshire, and had confirmed in respect to it the rights of the abbey of Westminster. Nor was the parent house forgetful of its obligations while it maintained its rights as patron. Guislebert, abbot of Westminster, conveyed to the Priory, with the assent of his Chapter, several manors and estates. Wolstan, Prior of Worcester, gave lands in Powyke, Bransford, and Leigh; and the great tithes of Powyke Church were in 1314 appropriated to Malvern by Walter de Maydesten. In the same way Upton Snodsbury was despoiled by Henry Wakefield to increase the income of Malvern. These gifts are only samples of an unfortunate system which prevailed in the Middle Ages, a system of impoverishing the parishes in order to enrich the monastic houses, and resulting in the just discontent of the secular clergy, and in anger, sometimes loudly expressed, among the laity. Much has been written of the spoliation of conventual revenues at the Dissolution, but we hear nothing of the injustice done to parishes which saw for generations their own revenues carried off to swell the opulence of some distant and (to them) alien institution. The Red Earl did better, for we believe it can be recorded that his considerable benefactions to the Malvern monks came from his own property and not out of the Church income of the parishes over which he was lord. So much may be put to his credit against, we fear, a heavy debit of oppressions under the forest laws. In parting from him it may be proper to mention that in addition to his long quarrel with the bishop of Hereford he had a dispute with bishop Gifford of Worcester, presumably on some boundary question, with the result that De Clare agreed to present the bishop with a couple of does, twice a year, at Kempsey. We may further say that his only son, and successor in the earldom, another Gilbert de Clare, fell at Bannockburn, leaving no issue, when the estate passed to his sister, Eleanor Despenser, in whose family it remained for some period, both as to the Chase and the castle.

We have noticed some of the many gifts which the Priory received for endowment, and undoubtedly it was growing in means and importance. But it must not be supposed that its history was altogether unclouded. On the contrary more than one misfortune befell it. The bishops of England looked with no little jealousy on the growth of the monastic orders, who were not amenable to their authority, and whose acquisitions had continually the effect of withdrawing property which ought to have remained under episcopal control. Thus more than one bishop of Worcester made determined efforts to extend his authority over Malvern Priory, and to oust the abbot of Westminster from his position as patron. Nor can it be denied that the bishops were justified in this object. Great as were the services which the monastic bodies, taken as a whole, rendered to the Church and the nation at a certain period of our history, it is also true that the independence which they enjoyed from episcopal authority was productive of disorders, and occasionally of calamity. This was unquestionably one of the grievances which brought about the final Dissolution. The fact may be and probably is denied by some ecclesiastical writers, whose eyes are blinded by natural prepossessions, but the truth is writ large in English history for those who study it with impartial care. We shall presently have to adduce a flagrant example. At the moment we may say that on more than one occasion about the close of the thirteenth century the bishop of Worcester succeeded in asserting his authority over the Priory, and the monks were driven to make over to him Knightwick, and also to yield, as it would appear, some other properties. But all this was protested against by the abbot and Chapter of Westminster, and was finally brought on appeal before King Edward the Second at York. That unfortunate monarch had retreated to York after his defeat by the Scots at Bannockburn, and it is probable that he remained in that city, then second only to London in its importance, until the question between the bishop and the abbot was brought up for his decision. The king finally gave judgement in favour of the abbey at Westminster, and its claim to the patronage of the Priory was thenceforth undisputed. Among other matters that came to light during this dispute it may be noted that the number of monks in the Priory was stated to be twenty-six, and moreover that some difficulty was felt in providing for their maintenance owing to the deprivation of property to which they had been subjected. It was also stated that the difficulty was increased inasmuch as they regularly supported thirty poor persons. It would seem then that this community, even when impoverished, did not neglect its duty of charity.[1]

[1] But see subsequent note.

But at this period a grievous scandal arose in the midst of its good works and devotion, a scandal which proved the necessity for some supervising hand to maintain a stricter discipline. The whole story is extraordinary, and would in some respects seem incredible were it not narrated by authorities whose accuracy can hardly be doubted. The Priory, it seems, had more than one subsidiary establishment, and among them a cell of four monks at Ledbury, a Herefordshire town not far from the western side of the Hills. We are not informed whether the John of Ledbury who played so conspicuous a part in the scandal with which we are dealing was a member of this cell, but it may be safely conjectured that he was so, and that his elevation to the post of Prior of Great Malvern was due to some supposed excellence in his qualities. That he was a bold man cannot be doubted, with a decision of character that might have done good service in any position, but as it turned out a capacity for evil which, when he had once taken a wrong turn, led him into enormities.

How soon after his elevation to the office of Prior he gave cause for complaint is not stated, but it appears that some effort had been made to restrain his proceedings before or about the time that the award was given by the Crown in favour of the abbey of Westminster. The Priory owned some land in the chapelry of Newland, and they had upon it a grange which had been built for agricultural purposes. In this dwelling John of Ledbury had established a harem of women, to the number of thirty or according to one account thirty-five, including among them his own sister, all of whom he apparently maintained out of the revenues of the Priory, for the purposes of his unholy life.[1] It is plain that such a state of things could not have been brought to pass in a day, it probably continued for some period, and it is difficult to picture to the mind the internal condition of the community. All we know is that this amazing head of a Benedictine Priory, bound by solemn vows to a life of chastity and devotion, was able not only to dominate his own monks but to set at nought all authority from without, and to hold his own within the fence of his convent. It is a strange picture of what was possible in those days, and confirms the opinion expressed above that the absence of episcopal authority over the monastic bodies not only could but did work mischief. As to the delay that

[1] Looking at the coincidence of the numbers in the two transactions, it is possible to conjecture that the thirty mistresses were the thirty objects of charity.

took place in dealing with John of Ledbury, it must be remembered that distance and difficulty of communication raised many obstacles. Assuming, as we probably may, that the abbot who was patron of the Malvern cell was the only person who could interfere with any effect, the long journey from Malvern to Westminster, and again from Westminster to Malvern, after much debate and hesitation, would account for a considerable time. Added to this the abbot could only use persuasion, which must have been thrown away, or at the most spiritual terrors, such as excommunication, which would be securely laughed at by the offender. A bishop acting within his diocese would have had officials and other ministrants, who might have shown themselves too strong for resistance, but how could an abbot, 120 miles away, vindicate his authority? Help, at length, came from the secular arm. The Chapter of Westminster were weak at Malvern, but they had influence at the seat of government, and we can hardly doubt that it was under their influence a writ was at last sent to the Sheriff of Worcestershire, directing him to call out the *posse comitatus* of the county, to march to Malvern and eject the contumacious Prior. That infamous creature had of course been already deposed by the

Chapter of Westminster, he was in illegal possession, and the sheriff had only to execute his orders. The knights and men-at-arms of the county were summoned to assemble on Powyke Ham, an open space about two miles from Worcester on the river Teme. The ancient bridge which still stands over the stream, though long disused, may perhaps have witnessed the gathering. All was ready for the march of six miles which would have taken them to the Priory, when it was learned that their services were no longer required. John of Ledbury, aware that the game was up, had the night before laid hold of the sacred vessels of the church, with anything else that was valuable, including of course any cash, had put them in a sack which he swung over his shoulder, had climbed the palisade of the convent in the darkness of the night, and made off across country, never to be seen again. Probably enough he crossed the Hills at the Wych, which was always one of the three passes, and was lost to pursuit, if any was attempted, in the woods of his own Herefordshire. He had had as a solitary monk the strange distinction of having compelled the whole county to arm against him, and of having taught a sad lesson that the best institutions are liable to disgrace if no adequate control is exercised over them.

Near to the close of the medieval period was fought the battle of Tewkesbury, within sight of the Malvern Hills, and owing its actual locality, as it happened, to their peculiar structure. There have always been during history, and probably were even when it was a submarine reef, three dips in the range: the Wych, near Great Malvern, where the lofty Worcestershire Beacon sinks to the level of the pleasant hills above the Wells; the Wind's Point above Little Malvern, where some ancient race thought the opening so important that they entrenched it strongly; and a third, the lowest and easiest of all, in Gloucestershire, not far from Tewkesbury. When Queen Margaret and her son landed in the south of England on their ill-starred expedition, their first object was to push forward into Wales, where the Lancastrian interest was strong. They were marching to Tewkesbury in order to cross the Malverns at the convenient pass we have last mentioned. It was a sound strategical move, and would probably have succeeded if they had been matched against an ordinary opponent. But the Queen, brave and resolute as she was, and supported by gallant adherents, had little chance when confronted with an adversary not inferior to Marlborough in vigour and rapidity of movement. Edward the Fourth, one of the greatest of a mighty line of warriors and statesmen, had just fought and won the battle of Barnet, where he had restored the fortunes of the White Rose. Without waiting for a day to recruit his troops or to celebrate his victory, and confident no doubt that he had crushed any possible danger of interference with his rear, he advanced at once by forced marches against the Lancastrian army, divined their plan in making for Wales, headed them before, though only just before, they reached Tewkesbury, and drove them to a fight. They were utterly routed, the Queen and her hapless son (soon to be murdered) were prisoners, and the campaign was ended. The Wars of the Roses had seen many surprising changes, but none perhaps so sudden and so brilliant as that wrought by Barnet and Tewkesbury. The misfortune was that never was victory, even in the rancour of civil war, more stained with cruel bloodshed. The scattered Lancastrians fled towards Tewkesbury with the victors close at their heels. A number of the fugitives took refuge in the great abbey church, invoking the protection of the altar. The abbot himself stood at the western entrance with the sacrament in his hand, and besought the pursuers to respect the sanctuary. But nothing would hold the

Yorkists; they rushed into the chancel, and there before the high altar they massacred their unresisting foes. There is a piece of ground in Tewkesbury called to this day the Bloody Field, and so called because within it were placed some hundreds of prisoners taken in the battle, to be murdered soon after in cold blood. Some writers have imagined that the name was given because the field was the site of the battle; but this is a mistake. The spot where the armies encountered, not very far from the town, is to this day plainly discernible by the small mound and surrounding trench where, as tradition has always told, Queen Margaret's standard flew. It may be added that the limits of the Bloody Field could not have sufficed for the two armies to stand together, still less to manœuvre and fight.

On this atrocious slaughter the Malvern Hills looked down. From any part of the range the tower of Tewkesbury Abbey is visible. It is still a noble structure, despite the wear of time and the hand of the spoiler. Built originally as a Norman church, in all the grand solidity that marked the style, it was afterwards altered to please the Decorated taste; an elaborate roof, marvellous in its carving, replaced the flat ceiling, and cut down the size of its clerestory windows. The apse was replaced by one of singular beauty in the then new style, and gazing at it, entranced, we feel forbidden to lament over the banished Norman, which now remains only in the lofty and massive pillars of the grand nave. The church was admirably restored in the closing years of the last century, and there are few in all England which bear more impressive testimony to the architectural genius of medieval England or to the manifold history which its ancient walls embody.

But we have now to turn to that Tudor period which not only delivered our country from the curse of civil war, but also opened out to it, through a series of surpassing events, the glories and the blessings of its more modern growth in strength and stature. In that development Malvern was to have its share.

V. TUDOR MALVERN

Bosworth Field closed for England a long chapter of trouble, and a new epoch opened when the crown, picked up from a bramble bush, was placed on the head of Henry the Seventh. The popular idea has always been fixed on that incident, but in truth the vital change had been settled some time before. Reginald Bray, a man of no ordinary ability, born within sight of the Malvern Hills, a native of St. John's suburb of Worcester, knew perhaps more than any one of the secret arrangements made for Henry's arrival and success. It happened that on a certain day he had been journeying on horseback from Worcester to Bridgnorth, and at no great distance from that town he met the Lady Margaret Tudor, who was riding to the west from Cheshire. She was acquainted with Bray, and they mutually stopped for a conference in what happened to be a conveniently secluded spot. Bray, it is believed, was Yorkist by conviction, but sick unto death of Richard the Third and his doings. To him, as to thousands, the blood of the murdered princes was crying from the ground. Lady

Margaret was a gifted and shrewd as well as a saintly woman, and she was not likely to lose her opportunity. She knew that Reginald Bray was a man of culture, able in his profession of the law, and well versed in the stormy politics of the day. An understanding was arrived at between them. Bray undertook to concert measures in support of a landing by Henry, and Lady Margaret solemnly covenanted that her son should marry the eldest daughter of king Edward the Fourth and thus secure the true York line of succession. The bargain was concluded (unlike some political bargains, it was faithfully carried out), and the two parties rode on to their respective destinations. The rest is matter of history, and there is no room for wonder that when Henry was firmly settled on the throne he made Sir Reginald Bray one of his foremost councillors.

But it is not with Bray's political career that we have to deal. For some reason unknown to us, he was deeply attached to the monastery beneath the Malvern Hills. It is possible that he there received his early education, before leaving for a university or the Inns of Court, from the Benedictine monks; but of course much more probable that he was taught at the school attached to the Priory of the same Order at Worcester. He may, however, as he grew older have visited the convent, have enjoyed the converse and society of the monks, have felt the magic of Malvern air, have climbed the hills at some of the easier points of ascent, and gazed on the woods and apple-orchards of Herefordshire, and on the blue distance of the Welsh mountains. But whatever the beguilement may have been, it is certain that his mind came to be bound up with Malvern, and that he never forgot its charm. The time arrived, in his days of advancement, when he showed his abundant affection.

Abbot Gasquet, in his interesting volume, entitled *The Eve of the Reformation*, has given an instructive account of the sort of craze which pervaded the country, in the later part of the fifteenth century, in favour of the new perpendicular style of architecture. Peace and prosperity were then increasing the wealth of the nation, the parish churches were the chief objects of popular interest, and on them the money acquired by trade and manufacture was laid out. Up to that time it had been the nobles and land-owners who had enlarged and decorated the churches; now it was the bulk of the people. Parish meetings were held, and resolved that the more ancient parts of the church should be removed and be replaced by the new and fashionable style. It is certain, we fear, that many valuable specimens of Early English work were swept away at this time, but it cannot be denied that the innovations effected were frequently superb. Always, we think, some portions of the old structure, and of course the best, were spared. It was a great movement of the people, born of an awakened taste, and animated by a religious spirit. Now what in parishes was done by the inhabitants was done for the Malvern conventual church by Sir Reginald Bray. For Bray was a highly accomplished man, and to his other attainments he joined a knowledge of and a taste for architecture which made him quite capable of designing and carrying out the erection of a great building. He has had attributed to him the completion of the beautiful Chapel of St. George at Windsor, a surpassing effort of the florid Gothic in its latest style. His architectural abilities have also been associated by tradition with the Chapel of Henry VII in Westminster Abbey. But in these matters there seems to have been some misapprehension. It is certain that both those celebrated works were executed by a well-known artist, Robert Vertue, though it seems that with regard to the former essential help was given by Bray, who supplied money and found labour. He is thus

MALVERN PRIORY CHURCH

undoubtedly entitled to some part of the credit. But as to the chapel of Henry VII Bray died at the time when that wonderful creation was just rising from the ground.[1] He did, however, enough to stamp him as a man well versed in the science of architecture, independently of the transformed church of the Malvern monks which stands to this day as his acknowledged work.

We have, in our remarks on Early Malvern, described the church as it was built when the monastery was founded; built in Norman style of somewhat rude character, but no doubt striking from its solidity. With this style Sir Reginald Bray determined to deal as so many parishes had dealt or were dealing with their churches; only perhaps more so. The choir and apse at the east end were demolished, and so was all else except the pillars of the nave and the door at the south-western corner which opened into the cloisters. These remain to this day in witness of the ancient structure. Above and beyond the relics of the old building was reared a magnificent perpendicular church, with all the tracery and decoration in which the ecclesiastical architects of the day revelled, high and

[1] *The Speakers of the House of Commons.* By Arthur Irwin Dasent. It may be noted that Sir Reginald Bray was Speaker in 1496.

expanded windows ornamented with carven stone and filled with glowing glass, a flat but lofty and panelled roof, two noble transepts, the northern of which was the Jesus chapel, two aisles, of which the southern contained St. Ursula's chapel, a fine porch, and a Lady chapel at the east end. This last, in common with the southern transept, has long since perished, but the foundations are still visible. The painted glass was remarkable, and a certain portion of it still remains, but disfigured by ignorant handling. The arms of several of the old families in the neighbourhood can yet be deciphered, and many scriptural subjects of course are represented. The dimensions of the church are 171 feet in length, 63 in breadth, and the height of the nave is 63 also. These are the figures given by Nash in his *Worcestershire*; the length of course is exclusive of the Lady chapel. Taken as a whole, when completed, with its carved seats for the monks, its encaustic tiles (some dated 1453) which paved and decorated the floor and walls, exhibiting the arms of England, and those of the abbey of Westminster, of Mortimer Earl of March, Bohun Earl of Hereford, Clare and Despenser Earls of Gloucester, the church must have been a wonderful sight, and one very different from that of the original structure, fine as that may have seemed in the period succeeding the Conquest. The building was throughout of New Red Sandstone, and the material was brought from a quarry not far from Bewdley, and carried down the Severn in barges to Clevelode, at the extreme eastern boundary of the wide parish of Malvern. From the river bank it was conveyed in wagons, probably drawn by oxen, through the district of the Chase now known as Barnard's Green, to the site of the church. The ancient quarry can still be seen, and those who care to look may remember that Malvern Priory church came out of it, and may bless the munificence of the large-minded Reginald Bray. His work lives after him. It is indeed a remarkable instance of the truth that no good deed wholly perishes. His original purpose was defeated three and a half centuries ago ; the choral hymn of the monks has long ceased to swell through the noble temple that he reared ; the community that he trusted would endure for ever under the shadow of the Hills has passed away ; but the church remains for the service of God and the spiritual welfare of Malvern, and those who enter it and have the intelligence to ponder on its history, should revere the memory of its founder, and breathe a prayer for the repose of his soul.

Of the buildings once belonging to the

Priory, other than the church, only one now remains. A new and handsome gateway to the monastic precincts was built by Bray, in the style which is now called Tudor, and exhibiting its well-known characteristics. It is of brick, faced with sandstone, and is peculiarly interesting from its situation no less than from its interior. For the gateway of the Priory must necessarily have faced both the village and the road by which it was approached from the plain below, and thus its situation, high above the church, proves that the village of Malvern had already, at the close of the fifteenth century, assumed the site it has ever since occupied, that being at the present moment the centre of the modern town. The population at that time was certainly small, but it must have been sufficient to ensure the due supply of conveniences, since even a royal visitor was accommodated at the Priory. The interior of the gateway, in the size of its apartments, and the scanty comfort which in every respect it displays, gives curious proof of the narrow ideas of the fifteenth century, at any rate as to habitation, compared with our own. For, small as are the dimensions of the rooms, confined altogether as is the space within the structure, there is no reason to doubt that Henry the Seventh and his minister, Sir

ANCIENT GATEWAY TO THE PRIORY PRECINCTS

Reginald Bray, occupied this gateway as the guests of the monks. Whether the visit was paid in order that the new church and buildings might be seen and admired, or whether the picturesque situation and the wonderful air of the Hills were the attractions, can now only be guessed. But the fact that such a visit was made may be taken as certain. The monarch who gave to England and to history the great line of Tudor sovereigns was the first royal visitor to Malvern, where no doubt he lived sumptuously on the red deer venison which the Chase supplied.

But there were other times coming. It is part of the cruel irony that appears to beset the fortunes of mankind that whether as individuals, communities, or nations, men never seem able to forecast their fate. In the beginning of the sixteenth century the wealth and the numbers of the religious orders in England were at their highest point. They had absorbed within the dead hand nearly 30,000 knights' fees, or about one-half of the number assigned by the Conqueror for the national defence ; in other words, nearly one-half of the landed property of the kingdom. No wonder that the laity had become alarmed, for there seemed no end to the process. But the 'religious' believed that the laity did not count in the matter, they were con-

†

fident that themselves would endure for ever and call the lands after their own names. Then just at the moment when they were most assured there came, as there usually comes after evils or inconveniences have long been growing, a confluence of circumstances undreamed of before, a sudden flood of change which no one man could have brought about, and no single event could have precipitated. It was not for nothing that a parliament of Henry the Fifth's earliest days had designed a raid upon the monasteries. That project had been adroitly shelved by a clerical suggestion of foreign war, and the subsequent remorse of Archbishop Chichele for his share in that transaction is in evidence at All Souls in Oxford. The idea of the Lancastrian parliament slept; but it awoke in more than its first vigour when a king, despotic by nature and powerful by passing circumstances, with a craving for money continually whetted by extravagance, headed the movement for curtailing the property of the monasteries. Of course the movement, as usual, went further than was originally purposed. The appetite for the lands grew as it was fed, and what had been started as a moderate reform passed into a sweeping confiscation. A fierce controversy has naturally raged on the subject, and with much exaggeration on both sides.

Amid a cloud of dispute some things are certain; one, that the swollen wealth of the 'religious' primarily brought on their downfall. Another, that it is useless to deny the existence of abuses. It is easy to say, or insinuate, that the reports of Henry's commissioners were untrue, and that tales of evil doings, at Fountains for instance, were invented to cover spoliation. No proof of this charge has ever been produced, and the probabilities are all against it. But what about the document to be seen in the library at Lambeth Palace? Is that a falsehood? It was compiled long before Thomas Cromwell was heard of; long before it was supposed that the younger son of Henry the Seventh would ever ascend the throne; long before the Dissolution was contemplated. It is a report on the infamous condition of the abbey of St. Albans and of an adjacent nunnery, prepared by Morton, archbishop of Canterbury, towards the end of the fifteenth century. Was the cardinal archbishop, Legate of the Pope, guilty of forging accusations against innocent monks and nuns? Of course not, it will be replied. Then would it not be better if zealous partisans, whether writing interesting tales or expounding dubious history, were to acquaint themselves with the Primate's terrible statements before commiting their pens to an unqualified defence of all religious houses in the sixteenth century?

On the other side it is unhistorical as well as unjust to argue from exceptional evils that the whole monastic system was rotten. An impartial survey of the facts must convince any genuine seeker after truth that the bulk of the religious houses were orderly and well-disposed, kind neighbours and good landlords, doing their duty conscientiously both in secular and spiritual matters. But in the great storm which swept over them the innocent perished with the guilty; the innocent many with the guilty few. Malvern Magna is an example of the unsparing nature of the revolution. It was not pretended that any accusation could be brought against that Benedictine community. The days of John of Ledbury were long past, and the monks had been, year after year, pursuing their quiet avocations, and practising their ready hospitality. Latimer was then bishop of Worcester; he can hardly be suspected of any papal leanings, but he protested against the destruction of the Priory. There is extant a letter of his to Thomas Cromwell, in which he pleads hard for its retention on the ground of the absolute need for some place of refuge in the wild and desolate country round the Malvern Hills. He moreover intimates that the Prior would be willing to pay a substantial sum to save the existence of his house. It was in vain. The convent which had received many a traveller besides royalty and its minister, which had sheltered men of science and philosophy, and done well for the people around it, was levelled with the ground, its property sequestrated, and, not least, its library dispersed or destroyed. The Benedictine monasteries were rich in manuscript books, many classical, some legal, others on interesting and various topics, and it was a grievous loss to the nation that so many of these literary treasures perished at the Dissolution. The spoliation in this instance was utterly unjustifiable, but the Priory of Malvern Magna only went the way of its parent house, though that, at any rate, became the Dean and Chapter of Westminster and perpetuated in another form the foundation and fame of its predecessor. In its new form it obtained a grant of some of the lands which had belonged to its 'cell', and it is believed that it still retains them. It may be mentioned that the income of Malvern Priory at the time of the Dissolution was given at £303 1*s.* 5½*d.* per annum. This of course represents some thousands at the present value of money.

There was another monastery on which

the Malvern Hills looked down. About four miles to the south along the range, at Little Malvern, there was a small community of monks, founded apparently by the Worcester Priory, a portion of whose church is still standing, having long been used as the church of the parish. It cannot be said that the character of this convent answered to that of Malvern Magna. The commissioners stated in their report that each of the few monks had a female companion living with him, and that the discipline of the place was altogether relaxed. The opinion of Henry Card, D.D., vicar of Great Malvern in the earlier period of last century, who had a deserved reputation as an antiquary, and to whose works the writer is indebted, is that no ground exists for impugning the verdict of the commissioners. And it must be remembered that in the case of a small and poor community there is the less reason for suspecting any invented accusation, seeing that the temptation in the way of property would have been meagre. There may have been a few gross scandals among the larger communities, but as a rule it was the smaller bodies of 'religious', being those attracting the least attention, who had broken their vows. We repeat something said before, that a lack of supervision is the explanation of much conventual history. The bishops had no power, and the Heads of the Orders were a long way off. What had been needed was a judicious reform; Wolsey saw this, and rightly began by getting rid of some smaller communities, and using their endowments for appropriate purposes. This policy, had it been carried out, would have both done much good and might have saved monastic institutions where they were needed and deserving. But the conception perished with the great Cardinal, and the flood that followed swept all alike away.

Thus the two convents of Great and Little Malvern, with very different characters, fell together. Each church became the parish church of its locality; that of Great Malvern to remain a stately structure; that of Little Malvern not much more than a picturesque ruin. The house which adjoins, however, exhibits considerable relics of the monastery, and must always be interesting to antiquarians. To the literary world the interest is still greater, for it is believed that a chance visit to the interior of Little Malvern Court, and the portrait of a monk in its dining-room, first inspired in the mind of J. Henry Shorthouse his wonderful tale of *John Inglesant.* All the surroundings of the place, the ruin of its sanctity, the beauty of its situation, the solemn tie that it maintains with the past, may well have affected the imagination of that gifted writer. But we quote the tradition without personally vouching for the fact. It may be added that the income of Malvern Parva at the Dissolution was £98 10*s*. 9*d*. The property was granted to one of the Russells of Strensham, and subsequently an Elisabeth Russell married Thomas Berington, in whose family it still remains. The number of monks was originally ten, but only six remained at the time of the Dissolution, and all six signed an acknowledgement of the king's supremacy.

The Priory buildings at Great Malvern were bestowed by the Crown on John Knotsford, Sergeant-at-Arms, and a tomb with the recumbent effigies of himself and his wife, placed between the chancel and the chapel of St. Ursula, commemorates their property in the church. But that was soon sold to the parish, whose own building had fallen into disrepair. That old parish church, which was dedicated to St. Thomas the Apostle, was situated to the north-west of the Priory. It was a small structure, ninety feet in length, and thirty-six in breadth, with one small chapel to the south. It was totally demolished when its successor was acquired. Of that only the chancel was used for divine service, the population being still small. In the fifth year of Elizabeth it amounted to 104 families. Malvern had reached this state at the end of the Tudor period, grown no doubt, but shorn of the institution which had for centuries been its ornament and stay.

The greatest sovereign of the Tudor line, the Queen who was the pride as she was also the bulwark of her country, was never at Malvern, though she was once very near it. She visited the city of Worcester, and must have seen the Hills as she rode through the county from the north; but she came no nearer to them. In the most memorable event of her glorious reign they were used for the same purpose as were other prominent heights. A fire was undoubtedly kindled on the Worcestershire Beacon, and probably four miles to the south on the Herefordshire Beacon also, to give warning of the approach of the Spanish fleet. A chance expression in Macaulay's fine ballad,

> Twelve fair counties saw the blaze from Malvern's lonely height,[1]

has given some added fame to the Hills. But this was the customary rhetoric of a poet, and will hardly bear examination. It is doubtful whether on the clearest day of

[1] Macaulay appreciated Malvern, and some of his letters, in the biography, are dated from it.

ordinary weather more than eight counties can ever be descried in that view, wonderful as it is, except on those rare occasions (a few perhaps in a century) when the veil of climate mist lifts from the Welsh mountains. This in broad sunshine. But what at night? A reply to this question was given in 1863, at the time of the marriage of the then Prince of Wales with his Danish bride. A bonfire was on that occasion lighted on the summit of the Worcestershire Beacon, and great expectations were entertained as to the distance from which its rays would be visible. As a fact the fire was seen from Worcester, but in a somewhat dim fashion, and it was seen in the same way on the Cotswolds, north and south, and of course over a considerable part of Herefordshire, probably also on the Clees. This would account for no more than five counties, and we may fairly consider that the number given in Macaulay's rhapsody must be halved to meet the real case. There is nothing in his words beyond the exaggeration permissible in all, especially in ballad poetry, of which the 'Lay of the Armada' is a brilliant example; but we are dealing here with plain facts. It must be remembered that the object of the ancient beacons was not so much to throw their light over an extensive area as it was to communicate with other similar fires, which thus handed on the alarm over the country. It is quite possible, however, that the art of arranging and encouraging the blaze was better understood in former times than it was in 1863.[1]

Anyway, it is worth recalling that the 'lonely height' of Malvern played its part in the great historical drama of that day—the high-spirited Elizabeth defying with 'foul scorn' the Spaniard's invasion of her realm.

[1] At the time when these pages were in the hands of the Oxford University Press the Coronation bonfire on the Worcestershire Beacon of the Hills was successfully lighted, and was clearly seen at various points in the north of the county.

VI. STUART MALVERN

There is an old ballad, quaint in character and versification, written by a vicar of Malvern in the reign of James the First. It cannot claim much praise for its poetical qualities, but it is valuable for the light which it throws on the social condition of the village. It shows that this had assumed a modern aspect, which marks indeed throughout England the change which had come about since the last and greatest of the Tudor line, the Queen beloved of her people, had passed away. The verses evince a religious spirit, but are rather in the fashion of a modern hymn, each ending with an exhortation to 'praise the Lord'. The vicar is evidently proud of his church, as he might well be, but his admiration is confined to 'its pillars stout and strong and windows large and long'; there is no glimpse of any appreciation of the noble architecture or the solemn antiquity. It is esteemed an excellent church for the parish, though not half of it is used for worship. Any eulogy a century earlier would, we think, have been more imaginative, perhaps more spiritual. But

INTERIOR OF MALVERN PRIORY CHURCH. 1607

there was something worse than want of appreciation, there had been ruinous want of care. A rare and curious engraving, of the date of 1607, is in existence, and portrays the interior of the Priory church as it was when the rhyming vicar wrote. From this engraving it appears that only the chancel was in use for service, and the nave, from which it was separated by a low partition, was empty. No doubt the chancel was ample in point of size for the small congregation which the village would then supply, but that could not excuse the lack of decent repair. The fine window at the east end is shown in a dilapidated condition, for on one side the ivy has entered through a gap in the glass, and the amount of growth spreading over the stone tracery is sufficient proof of past years of neglect. The whole aspect of the place is desolate, and a glance at the empty nave, with its pavement damp and bare, speaks of nothing but disuse and decay. To this state the great Tudor church had sunk in a couple of generations, and its accredited guardian could boast of its windows and pillars without a thought for their preservation.

But then the song goes on, and the ancient Chase is dealt with. The 'royal deer' are there as in former days, but their advantage to the inhabitants is thought questionable;

there are too many of them; they are more a matter for resignation than for pride;

> Yet, though they eat away
> Thy corn, thy grass, thy hay,
> Do not forget, I say,
> To praise the Lord.

This was a great falling off in sportmanlike feeling, not to say in loyalty, from the time of the Red Earl. Yet royal forests were still in use in England. There is a tale that when the Muscovite ambassador made himself obnoxious by his rude behaviour, Elizabeth sent him to hunt the wild boar in the wood of St. John. At Weybridge, where the picturesque heights of St. George's Hill are now the sole relics of the forest which formerly covered that part of Surrey, an empty shell of what was once a giant oak marks the spot where the Queen narrowly escaped death from a stag at bay, only saved by the devotion of her huntsman who perished himself on the animal's horns. The incident is pictorially represented on a brass in the church of Walton-on-Thames. James the First, too, hunted the deer in the royal parks near London, but, according to Walter Scott, in a more timorous fashion than did Elizabeth. As no mention is made of sport in the lyric we are considering, it may be supposed that it was not pursued with much activity. What we really learn from the Vicar's lines is that in the early part of the seventeenth century Malvern Chase existed in unimpaired extent, though probably there had been internal enclosures, as for instance at Blackmore. The forest laws were still in force, but it is not likely that they were administered with rigour, and on the other hand the inhabitants of the parishes within the limits of the Chase were entitled to commonable rights as to wood and pasture.

On another point the information given by this scrap of literature is interesting. It appears that the purity of Malvern water was looked upon as curative, and that numbers came, even from distant places, to obtain its benefits. They lay about, no doubt beside the rivulet from St. Anne's Well, and were cured of divers affections, 'ulcers' and 'bruises' are particularly mentioned, by using the stream. It may be fairly conjectured that this was no new thing. From the days of Aldwin, when the well had first been esteemed holy, there had been visitants to its clear waters and the invigorating breezes around. Those qualities had not departed with the monks, and cures, quite as miraculous as any which religion had blessed in other days, were now wrought by simple food, daily climbing, pure water and good air. Perhaps it is more astonishing to learn that the trade in Malvern water which goes on briskly, we believe, at the present day, was active in the reign of the first Stuart. The author from whom we have quoted recites, as the concluding triumph of his little rhapsody, that the waters of his parish are dispatched in various directions, the heralds of health to people afar, and he ends with the benediction,

> Some of them into Kent,
> Some are to London sent,
> Others to Berwick went,
> Oh praise the Lord!

One could not invent, if one wished to do so, a more complete proof of the modernity to which the ancient village on the Hills had now attained.

But the time was not far distant when a still greater change was to come to pass. King James had in 1625 been succeeded by his son, and Charles, whatever his shortcomings as a ruler may have been, had undoubtedly a desire and taste for practical improvements in the condition of the country. There were royal domains, other than that of Malvern Chase, given up of old to sporting purposes, and which had become useless wastes. One of these was the Isle of Axholme, on the borders of Lincolnshire and Yorkshire, a wilderness of wood, marsh, and mere, haunt only of deer and wild-fowl. Charles determined that it should be drained and reclaimed for cultivation, and for this purpose he engaged the services of Cornelius Vermuyden, a Dutch engineer. That able man, versed in the art which had made his country, constructed a number of deep channels in the Isle to carry off the superfluous water, doing his work with great skill in the teeth of violent opposition from the people of the neighbourhood. Harriet Martineau, in one of her charming tales, has perpetuated the history of his enterprise. His difficulties of course were much increased by the fact that he had imported some hundreds of Dutch workmen with their families, whose descendants still remain on the soil, distinguishable to this day for their respectability, independence, and remarkable cleanliness. They brought over, it may be told in passing, their Dutch pastor, a learned man who settled in the Isle, and became the intimate friend of Samuel Wesley, vicar of Epworth, father of an illustrious son. It may fairly be conjectured that the Arminian opinions of the founder of the Wesleyan Communion, opinions so widely different from those of his present followers, came from this Dutch source.

Charles was well pleased with Vermuyden, knighted and otherwise rewarded him. And when it was resolved that Malvern Chase also should be reclaimed to cultivation, he made a grant to Richard Heath and Sir Cornelius Vermuyden of one-third of that royal domain, themselves undertaking to effect the reclamation. The remaining two-thirds were given to the parishes which had common rights for wood and pasture. It does not appear that the old forest regulations were interfered with, perhaps they were reserved for royal exercise. This kingly procedure, in which the rights and benefit of the people at large were disregarded in a truly Stuart fashion, was deeply resented. Disturbances broke out at Hanley Castle and other places, and became so menacing that the King in Council, on the 12th of May, 1631, declared the whole Chase free of the forest laws, and confirmed the rights of the freeholders in the various parishes to their usages and 'estovers'. This was in effect the end of Malvern Chase in its feudal character, but it was long before the design of the king was fully carried out. What became of the two grantees; what profit, if any, they reaped from their third share of the domain, does not anywhere appear.[1] Probably, after expenses paid, it was

[1] But Sir Cornelius Vermuyden appears again at

moderate enough, and in this, as in other matters, Charles was unfortunate in his undertakings because his finance was weak. But it may be presumed that the deer were improved off the face of the country, with no small benefit to the cultivators. In more than one district the ascertained dates of the older houses show that they were built soon after the disafforesting proclamation. An old house at Barnard's Green, for instance, has been rated in the parish books since 1635, and there was, near it, not many years since, a yeoman's habitation, freehold property, occupied by his forefathers in unbroken succession from at least some years before the outbreak of the Civil War. These are conclusive proofs that the work of reclamation made some progress. But the confusion that followed the hostilities between Charles and his Parliament put an end to this as to other contemplated improvements. Civil war is, of all wars, the most inimical to civilization, and it was not till after the Restoration that the reclaiming process was resumed. An Act entitled for the further disafforesting

the time of the Commonwealth, when he seems to have suggested to Cromwell a project for a close, if not a corporate, union between England and the United Provinces. Vermuyden was employed by Cromwell to negotiate with the Dutch for some such purpose, but the proposal came to nothing.

of Malvern Chase was then put upon the Statute Book, and thus a final end came to the royal forest created 500 years before. Since then the Malvern Hills have looked down on a marvellous growth alike of industrial production and of population, urban and rural.

The military operations during the war that raged from Edgehill to Naseby could hardly have touched the Hills, unless it were by the passing of troops of either party, in the one direction or the other, through that easy pass across the range near to Tewkesbury which had been aimed at by Queen Margaret's Lancastrian army.[1] But in the second war, when the young and adventurous Charles made a dash from Scotland for his English crown, the conflict not only came within sight of the Malvern Hills, but at one point very near to them. The relief of the siege of Madresfield Court fitted in with Cromwell's strategy. Charles Stuart, as he then was, a Pretender, at least as far as England was concerned (he had been crowned King of Scotland), was in possession of Worcester, with an army composed mainly of Scotchmen but recruited with Eng-

[1] In the earlier years of the war there had been skirmishes between the opposing forces at Powyke, two miles from Worcester.

lish cavaliers, more especially from Worcestershire. If Charles could reach Wales he might reasonably expect further reinforcements, or if he could hold Worcester and command both banks of the Severn his Welsh adherents could easily join him. Both these possibilities were open at the time, both no doubt were perceived by Cromwell, and he devised an able plan to meet the emergency. He marched from the south on the left bank of the Severn, thus blocking the further advance of Charles into England. When this march brought Cromwell to or near Pershore he sent Lambert, one of his generals of division, on a cross-country expedition towards Upton-on-Severn, with orders to pass the Severn at Upton and to make his way towards Worcester on the right bank. Now it happened that Lambert's way after forcing Upton bridge, which he did by a fierce but brief onset, led him near to Madresfield Court, the ancient seat of the Lygon family, who were then as they had long been and were long after, stout Whigs and Parliamentarians, and consequently obnoxious to the royalists. When therefore the invading army arrived at Worcester, a party was dispatched to seize Madresfield Court. But that turned out to be less easy than was supposed. The Lygon of the day was not a man to submit tamely; he called in his tenants and retainers and resolved to fight. The house, which is highly interesting as a sample of what the habitations of the country gentry were when castles went out of fashion as cumbrous and uncomfortable, but when some form of defence was still desirable, was then, as it still is, moated and sufficiently solid to stand some battering. As a fact, not a few houses of this kind sustained a considerable siege during the Civil War. Outside it there was a fine avenue of elms which Lygon cut down to form barricades. The moat was at that time furnished with a drawbridge, and beyond the moat was a pair of stout oak doors, known as the old doors, and beyond them again at the end of a vaulted passage was another pair, known as the new doors. These latter were of the reign of Henry the Eighth, the former were certainly as old as the Conquest, probably older, for the Lygon family was of Saxon date. With a deep moat around and massive gates beyond it the house, barring famine, might have held out for some time. But Lambert's advance of course raised the siege. The royalist party at once retreated to Powyke, where they vainly endeavoured to hold the bridge over the Teme, which was forced after a short skirmish and its defenders driven back to Worcester. Lambert followed them promptly, occupied the suburb of St. John, and thus sealed up the exit from Worcester bridge. Cromwell's strategy had succeeded completely. Any advance to the south, any retreat to or communication with Wales, were equally blocked; the royalist army was caught in a trap, with Cromwell on one side close to the walls of the city, and Lambert on the other in command of the Severn. The issue of the campaign was clear.

But Lambert was too able a soldier to leave anything doubtful. During the night following his occupation of St. John's he contrived to throw a bridge of boats across the Severn near the spot where the Teme joins that river, and the next day he was in communication with his great commander and in a position to assist him. Cromwell was at that time close before Worcester, with his right flank on Perry Wood, and his left extending in the direction of the Severn. The royalists on their part had not been idle. They knew that the city itself was indefensible, for its southern walls were commanded by the heights above Sidbury, and on those heights was the enemy. With much energy they constructed on the top of Sidbury hill a strong earthwork, and resolved to hold it to the last extremity. Some remains of this redoubt are still to be seen, and mark at once the crisis and the slaughter of the fight. Cromwell's dispatch shows clearly that the fighting was desperate on this spot, and that the event seemed for a time doubtful. The Worcestershire cavaliers fought like lions, in marked contrast with the lukewarm behaviour of the Scotch troops.[1] But Lambert was at hand; he crossed the river with his division, marched up the slopes above, fell on the right flank of the royalists, and finished the fight. Fort Royal was carried, its defenders and in fact the whole of Charles's army were driven pell-mell into the city and never rallied. Charles, who had shown much gallantry, rode for his life, but when he had passed through Sidbury gate he found that the street was blocked by a wagon of hay, which had been overturned there to stay the pursuit. He had to abandon his horse, and then managed to crawl through the hay. When he emerged on the other side there was a cry for some one to mount the king; a gentleman in New Street, close by, brought out his horse saddled, and Charles mounted. He went along New Street and made his

[1] The Dean had preached, on the Sunday, a furious sermon against Presbyterians. Charles may have said, 'Save me from my friends.'

way out of Worcester by St. Martin's gate, riding with a few companions in his flight. They halted at Barbourne, about a mile outside the city, where a small brook crosses the road, and there Charles held his last council of war. It was, after a hurried consultation, determined that they should separate and that each man should shift for himself. Charles, upon that, rode up the county through Droitwich and Feckenham, with intent to reach Staffordshire.[1] It is well known that he there narrowly escaped capture, and that he thence made his way through a hundred dangers down to the south coast, and embarked in an open boat, at a spot not far from Shoreham, to find safety in France. It is only just to a man whose character, on divers grounds, has been much assailed, to remember that during the whole of his perilous flight he exhibited a rare courage, and that he was more than once saved by his own personal coolness.

The battle of Worcester was fought within sight of the Malvern Hills, and may fairly be claimed as an incident of their history. From their summits the tower of Worcester Cathedral is plainly visible, and from the

[1] On his way, while still in Worcestershire, he was joined by Wilmot, who probably had ridden up at first by the Kidderminster road.

hill on which Fort Royal stood their lovely outline is absolutely clear. They had seen the last bloodshed in the Wars of the Roses, and they now witnessed the last mortal fight between an ill-fated dynasty and a Parliament resolute for its ancient privilege. And so, after some thirty more troublous years, the Stuart period passed away, for the Malvern Hills and for all England beside.

VII. GEORGIAN MALVERN

THE reigns of the Georges are usually thought uninteresting. Certainly there were none of the intestine wars or changes of dynasty which we read of in earlier times. Two efforts indeed were made to alter the succession to the throne, but the first failed so completely that the aspirant, though he was off the coast, never ventured to land; and the second, after a gallant effort, closed in crushing disaster. In effect the Stuart drama was played out. On the other hand there has been no period in our history more fertile in literature and few more active in social progress than that of the Georges. The Georgian architecture may have been solid and stiff, and the Georgian manners formal. But we may not have improved upon either. Nor in regard to military glories or colonial expansion can it be truly said that we have much surpassed the Georgian days.

The history of Malvern in those days was quiet, but not uneventful. The growth of population was slow. In an early year of Queen Elizabeth, as we have seen, it was returned as a little over 100 families; in the time of Nash, the historian of Worcestershire, at the close of the eighteenth century, it was given as 120 families. It was still, of course, a country village. In 1711, when good Queen Anne was reigning, a citizen of Bristol, one William Williams, was taken with the idea that the Hills could be profitably mined. It is possible that the glitter of the mica which is found in the syenitic rock deceived him and perhaps others into the belief that gold might be discovered. Copper ore, it would seem, was also expected. The science of geology was then unknown; it was not till near a century later that William Smith, of Churchill in Oxfordshire, a rough and not highly educated man, but with the vigour and persistence of genius in his blood, tramped over a large part of England to note the positions and characteristics of the various strata, and made himself famous as the father of British geology. He would have laughed at the notion of finding gold or any other metal in the Malvern rocks, but the Bristol speculator had no such adviser. Williams sank a pit on the side of the Hills, and was so confident of success that he persevered for ten years in his visionary effort. It was in 1721, after spending according to Nash a substantial sum of money, that he finally abandoned the diggings, which of course were never resumed. It is curious now to remember that there was always a secret, more precious than gold to those who desire knowledge, lying hid under the then impenetrable Hills, the secret, as already related, of their submarine origin, reaching back to what would have appeared to Georgian ears incredible antiquity.

The Bristol enterprise cannot have brought much profit to Malvern, beyond raising perhaps at the time the value of labour in the neighbourhood, but there was a man coming who was destined to alter the fortunes of the village on the Hills. John Wall was born in 1708, the son of a prosperous Worcester tradesman, who had been mayor of the city; and the boy was well educated in the cathedral school, where the great John Somers first showed his intellect. From that foundation John Wall was elected a scholar of Worcester College, Oxford, where he won a reputation in the University, became a friend of several men of eminence, and was in a few years chosen a Fellow of Merton College. Even in his early boyhood he had shown a passion for painting, so much so that when his father died and the Lord Sandys of that day became his guardian, the latter was so concerned lest constant use of the oil colours should affect his ward's health that he forbade the occupation. But it was soon resumed when the young artist became his own master. In compliment to Merton he designed and executed, for its hall, a large historical composition, representing the founder in episcopal robes and mitre, pointing to a view of his college ; some allegorical figures were introduced, and two cherubs held a scroll containing the names of distinguished members of Merton, among them being Roger Bacon, Linacre, and Harvey. This painting, which disappeared from the hall, no one knows how, in the earlier part of last century, was of course in a style now out of date ; but it must have been well executed, and was certainly a remarkable production for a self-taught hand. This peculiarity was commemorated by the inscription on the canvas : 'J. Wall, αὐτοδίδακτος Inv. pinx. 1765.' Long before this, and in fact soon after he had taken his B.A. degree, Wall addicted himself to the study of medicine, which was no doubt congenial to his philosophical and inquiring mind. He pursued this branch of knowledge both at Oxford and at St. Thomas's Hospital, and in 1736 he was admitted to the degree of Bachelor of Physic. In 1739 he graduated as Doctor of Medicine, settled as a consulting physician at Worcester, and married Catherine Sandys, first cousin of the peer. He soon became, and remained for some thirty years, the head of his profession in Worcestershire.

It was then that his connexion with Malvern, and the benefits that he conferred upon it, came to pass. Do not let it be supposed that the account given above of John Wall's natural aptitudes is out of place. On the contrary, it was his high education and his peculiar gifts which made him the benefactor and embellisher of the ancient village on the Hills. Why it was that the fashion prevalent, as we have seen, in the time of James the First of using the Malvern waters for the cure of injury and disease, had died out as it seems to have done, is not to be explained. It is only certain that, after a century perhaps of oblivion, the perceptive mind of Dr. Wall fastened on the subject, that he brought his scientific knowledge to bear, and was the first to point out with authority the peculiar purity and hence the health-giving properties of the water on the Hills. Those qualities had been known in earlier times, but known only in an empirical way. It was he who analysed the flow from the springs which had in ancient days been esteemed holy, and showed that they were absolutely free from all organic matter. The results thus obtained he published in a tract, which was wittily summarized in a couplet:

> The Malvern water, says Dr. Wall,
> Is famed for containing just nothing at all.

That perfect purity has been from of old its characteristic. It springs from the igneous rock, a virgin supply from unpolluted sources, sources that originated in a past not to be computed in figures, when the submarine reef was formed under volcanic heat, and pushed upward by earthquake force. But this description applies only to the two springs situated high on the Hills, St. Anne's and the Holy Well. There is a third spoken of by Dr. Wall, chalybeate, which is on the lower slope, issuing from the sandstone. This is little heard of nowadays, indeed we doubt if it is at all frequented, but it is said in his tract to be a valuable curative for certain disorders, though he found that it contained only a small quantity of iron. His *Experiments and Observations on the Malvern Waters* may still be worth reading, and whatever opinion the medical science of to-day might pass upon its pages, it is certain that to Dr. Wall the fame of Malvern as a watering-place in the eighteenth century is wholly due. But he did more than this; he was the author of its modern capabilities. Here the original qualities of his mind and character came into play. His artistic taste, kept alive and ardent by the pursuit of painting in every available hour, made him keenly conscious of the picturesque. He must have been as deeply in love with Malvern scenery as he was appreciative of Malvern springs and air, and under this impulse he planned and carried out walks on the Hills to enable visitors to enjoy the views. This was more especially the case at Malvern Wells, some three miles south of Malvern proper, where the easy and delightful terraces leading gradually on and upwards are the solace of all who enjoy a little peaceful exercise. He also exerted himself to further in that sweet seclusion the erection of more than one boarding-house which aided for wellnigh a century the prosperity of the place. In all this he was the real father of the modern Malvern ; his genius and taste inspired its character, which retained for long the stamp of aristocracy. He has met with the usual fate of gifted men. You may now walk the length of the Hills without finding a person who has heard of his name.

But fortunately his fame found another monument, and one that is bound up with the history of the Georgian period. The success of Charles Edward Stuart in Scotland in 1745, and his subsequent advance into England, futile as that march proved to be, caused keen anxiety among the Whig party. It was made obvious that while the sober sense of the nation at large approved of the existing dynasty, there was little enthusiasm in its favour. Many efforts were made both in London and in the country to remedy this state of things, and Dr. Wall, who was an ardent Whig, came forward in the cause. At that time the Dean and Chapter of Worcester Cathedral were Jacobite in tendency, and greatly influenced political opinion in the city. Dr. Wall resolved on founding a new industry in support of Whig principles. Many years since Mr. Gladstone, a great authority on china, as he was on so many other matters, pointed out in a remarkable speech at the Athenaeum Club that the establishment of the porcelain manufacture at Worcester was due to a political motive. That is absolutely true, but it may be added that its success was also due to the perceptiveness as well as the energy of Dr. Wall. Just as he had discovered the peculiar qualities of the Malvern waters, so his quick eye and power of observation perceived in Cornwall the particular clay best fitted for the making of fine porcelain. He was not content with sight or conjecture, but carried out a careful investigation bychemicalexperiment, and his opinion in favour of the material to be used holds good to the present hour. He went further, and founded a company which supplied the necessary capital, purchased a site for the new works close to the cathedral precincts, and in 1751 saw the enterprise started to its world-wide success. There is not a doubt that it was to his fine and cultivated taste that the beauty of the old Worcester china, both in colour and design, was due. The early products of the manufacture sprang direct from his wonderful brain. At this day the best recommendation of 'Old Worcester' is that it shows 'Dr. Wall's blue'. So in truth what had been his boyhood's passion, and the recreation of his vigorous manhood, influenced also the most remarkable achievement of his life. Taken as a whole, with his painting genius, his inventive faculty, and his professional success, he was assuredly one of the most eminent of the men who have lived under the shadow of the Malverns.

The ancient church of Great Malvern, the mother of its civilization, and the guardian for centuries of its welfare, did not share in the growing prosperity of the place. It had become the parish church, but was far too spacious for the purpose, and its maintenance must have been a heavy burden for an ordinary village with an area around it scantily populated. We have already told of the desolation and neglect into which it had fallen early in the seventeenth century. The eighteenth was not likely to do better. Full of activity and renown in many departments of life, it did not breed restorers or preservers of churches. It is lamentable to think of the amount of priceless glass, priceless because no art now existent can recall its colouring and quality, which perished through wind and weather, under the hands of schoolboys who cared only to hear the crash as their missiles burst on 'the prophets blazoned on the panes', and under, it may well be, the pilferings of curious beholders. There was of old, in the Jesus chapel of Malvern Church, a wonderful window, of which the upper part was filled with representations of sacred subjects, taken from Scripture or from medieval imaginings. In the lower part were the figures of Henry VII armed and crowned with an imperial crown; on his upper garment the arms of France and England; behind him Elizabeth, his queen, with the same arms on her garment; behind her Arthur, Prince of Wales, likewise armed; behind him Sir Reginald Bray bearing on a shield argent a chevron between three eagles; behind him John Savage and Thomas Lovell: all kneeling and bearing palm branches lifted up to heaven; with this inscription: *Orate pro bono statu nobilissimi et excellentissimi regis Henrici septimi et Elizabethe regine et domini Arthuri principis filii eorundem, necnon pro dilectissime consortis sue, et suorum trium militum.* This beautiful window, says Dr. Nash, after giving the above description, was perfect in the year 1720, but soon after a violent storm blew it down, and, being very much broken, an ignorant glazier misplaced the pieces that were left. The reader may be interested to observe that the above account confirms what has been previously said of the interest taken by Henry VII and Reginald Bray in the Priory church. The mention of the imperial crown is historically valuable, because it supports the contention narrated by an old writer to have been made successfully, on a diplomatic occasion, in the reign of Henry VI, that England was no part of the continental empire, but had an independent sovereignty. So does the name of Prince Arthur remind us that the ashes of that promising heir to the Tudor throne, cut off in his early youth, repose in a chapel of Worcester Cathedral. The mention of his consort shows that he was already married to Katherine of Aragon when the window was painted. But all this interest is merged in lamentation that such a window, bearing such a record, should have been sacrificed by the ignorance or carelessness of its accredited guardians. It is of small credit to our Malvern Hills history that what the Tudor period so lavishly produced, the Georgian period should have so heedlessly cast away.

But now, now that a great sorrow has been succeeded by a great hope, we must not forget that the line of the Georges, decried as it has been by some cynical writers, and open it may be in occasional passages to sober criticism, has restored its name, has renewed its life, and will assuredly perpetuate its glory. George the Fifth, whom may God preserve, has no need to regard his predecessors with aught but pride. George the First came here, as the good Duke of Sussex once said, 'to secure the liberties of the people', a mission which the dynasty has fully and patriotically performed. On the field of Dettingen George the Second upheld, with heroic resolve, at once the balance of power in Europe and the honour of the British flag. Under his victorious sceptre Wolfe added Canada to the empire and Clive won India at a stroke. George the Third 'gloried in the name of Briton', set an example of manly morality, and stood steadfast to his country's cause through triumph and adversity alike. George the Fourth, whatever his errors or mischances, was a courtly and august sovereign. We ask no better dynasty, we seek no higher auguries. May the great line with which we are blessed by Providence 'stretch out to the crack of doom'!

VIII. VICTORIAN MALVERN

Each of the historical periods through which we have hitherto traced the legend of the Malvern Hills embraced several reigns and was marked by various changes of policy. That one at which we are now arrived, and the last with which we shall trouble our readers, is marked with a single name which pervades its whole story, the name of Victoria. That truly royal lady identified the period of her rule with her own personality in a way that few sovereigns have ever done; her letters and writings, and no less her character, have stamped her image upon memory in all parts of her wide empire. But to Malvern the name of Victoria had a peculiar significance, for she was known there when as a child she was little known to the kingdom at large, and she trod its Hills, heiress presumptive to the throne of her ancestors, yet without any state or show, and perhaps not more than dimly conscious of her future destinies. It was indeed in the summer of 1831, amid all the tumult of the first Reform Bill agitation, that the Princess, then twelve years of age, came to Malvern with her mother. She and the Duchess occupied Hollymount, which was vacated for their convenience by its owner, Lieutenant Thomas Woodyatt, R.N., while the adjoining property, the Lodge, accommodated the Master of their Household, Sir John Conroy, with his family. Hollymount, long since ruined by the constant curse of picturesque localities, the speculative builder, was at that time a charming residence. Absolutely secluded, with a wide view over the Severn plain below to the far Cotswolds and even (in gaps) beyond them, with embowering woods to shelter it behind, gardens and grounds skilfully laid out, and the divine air of the Hills breathing around, there was little left to desire. A taste for Italian art had done much for the inside of the house. Here the royal visitors remained for some period, climbed the Hills which then preserved much of a simple beauty, now long since bereft, and saw something of the surrounding country. Malvern was then a pretty village, set down among wooded fields and rural pleasantness. Beyond the ancient gateway of the Priory (then misnamed the Abbey) there were only four houses, the three of Abbey Place and the old Abbey Boarding House which occupied part of the site of the conventual buildings, and contained some relics whose antiquity has not saved it from destruction. Looking through the gateway from the north, orchards and green fields were visible. Graham Road was not then laid out, and on the slope to the east, just where the descent now turns to the railway station, there stood that sure mark of rural life, a turnpike. But some few innovations were in progress, and among them Foley Walk had just been constructed, leading from the Wych Road (then barely begun) to close upon the spot where Aldwin the hermit made his first abode. This new walk was much admired, and the Princess was asked to open it. She, or more probably the Duchess of Kent on her behalf, graciously consented. It must have been a pretty sight as the young girl, with childish grace, though even then with some of the dignity that became the heir of a line of kings, moved along the path. An officer of the Army who had served with his regiment in India, and had (it was believed) suffered somewhat in his head from India's sun, walked backwards before her, scattering flowers. He was living at the time, after the same eccentric vein, in the ancient gateway, occupying the rooms which had once housed Henry VII and Sir Reginald Bray. His courtly performance excited a little amusement, but the company which

HENRY CARD, D.D., VICAR OF GREAT MALVERN
FROM 1815 TO 1844

on that occasion thronged Foley Walk was of a kind now little seen in Malvern, and high caste gave nothing but a passing smile to harmless vanity. This was one of the few occasions on which the Princess was allowed to appear in public. Traditionary stories were long told about various incidents concerning her, but these have now passed beyond verification.

The vicar of Malvern at that time was Henry Card, D.D., a man of no ordinary attainment, and he probably saw more of the royal party than any other inhabitant. We have heard, but do not vouch for the fact, that on the recommendation of the historian Hallam, Dr. Card was consulted as to the historical studies of the Princess. He was well fitted to advise, for his researches had been directed into the earlier and least understood periods of English constitutional learning. In addition to this he was no mean antiquarian, and well versed in the ancient story of the Priory, its early inhabitants and its later enlargement and decoration. It was to him that the preservation of the church from decay was mainly due. We have more than once mentioned the partial ruin into which the majestic fabric had at one time fallen. The rare engraving of 1607 shows that in some seventy years after the

Dissolution the aspect of the interior was one of desolation. More than two hundred years had passed since then, and little if anything, or anything substantial, had been done to repair, while time had been busy with its destroying hand. At any rate, it is certain that when Dr. Card became vicar the church was threatened with collapse. He devoted himself to its preservation, and for many years unweariedly pursued the task. The first thing to do was to arrest the process of destruction, and for this purpose the roof was made secure and the rain no longer poured in. The windows were repaired, and every care was taken to prevent any further damage to the stained glass. The north aisle, and also St. Ursula's chapel, were put in repair, and the Jesus chapel, still suffering from the disaster in 1720, was well secured. The main difficulty was the want of funds. It was always a poor benefice, for the monks had at an early period appropriated the great tithes, and when those were allotted to private owners at the time of the Dissolution it was but a comparatively scanty pittance that remained for the vicar of the large parish after providing the inevitable curate. The chief resource was the visitors, who increased in number when and after royalty had visited the village. This means of supply was indefatigably worked by Dr. Card, who left no stone unturned to rouse an interest in the work of restoration. One lady there was among his parishioners who did him good service, a person rather remarkable from her age and character, Apphia Lady Lyttelton. She belonged to more than one century, must have lived through more than two generations, and in her prolonged old age was the most prominent inhabitant of the parish. The Lyttelton schoolroom, built by her bounty, stands in the churchyard, and it was only one of the benefits which she conferred upon the place. She supported the vicar continuously in his efforts to preserve the church, and her name deserves to be held in lasting honour. It cannot be pretended that the work of restoration was always carried out in an entirely faultless way. The days of Professor Willis and Sir Gilbert Scott, the one to expound the architecture of our ancient churches, the other to show in what reverential way their renovation could be effected, had not then come. But at any rate one great end was achieved ; the fabric was made safe, a decent reparation was done throughout, full accommodation was provided for the congregations which filled the long nave in the summer season, and a foundation was laid for further improvement when fuller knowledge and more abundant means should be forthcoming. And this saving work, now of course forgotten, was done by Henry Card. The time came when the full purpose was carried out, when the church was cleared of much that encumbered it, and the original plan of its architecture, though of course sadly marred by past desecration, was made plain to the eye. Some regrets must be felt. The south transept was not rebuilt; and it was unfortunate that those engaged in the business of restoration substituted the name of St. Anne for that of St. Ursula, to whom ancient piety had dedicated the chapel in the south aisle. Such outrages on the past have been too common in our churches; whatever else they may be, they cannot be called restoration. But saving this, and it may be some other mistakes, the reparation effected in the later Victorian period did credit to the Malvern which had by that time grown richer as well as more populous.

There is one name connected with the Hills in their former days which will live in literature. Elizabeth Barrett was born in a Herefordshire house which looked towards the western side of the range, and her young mind was much occupied with its beauties and permanently affected by their influence. That will not be doubted by any who remember

INTERIOR OF MALVERN PRIORY CHURCH, 1911

her lines on 'Gorse from the Malvern Hills', which she wrote many years after she had parted from her home, wrote in a distant land and in sickness. The yearning for a sight of the scenery which had fed her childhood's imagination is breathed in every word. The Hills may be proud of her memory, for she was perhaps the first Englishwoman who wrote poetry of the higher kind, poetry that may be placed beside the verse of great writers and not suffer from the comparison. Nor is it the least part of her fame that she gave domestic happiness to one of the greatest poets of the Victorian age. Neither, as we are speaking of celebrities, let it be forgotten that in one of the most romantic spots of the Hills whose story teems with mystery and wonder, close under the trenches of an earthen stronghold whose makers and whose object no man can explain with certainty, there lived for years and ultimately died one of the sweetest and most poetical singers of Victoria's reign. Jenny Lind delighted in the air of the Malvern Hills, and she passed to rest under their shadow.

There was another lady who in the early Victorian days added some interest to the neighbourhood. Those who are acquainted with the amusing diaries of Madame D'Arblay (Fanny Burney) may remember her mention of the young child of Mrs. Dewes who was in her room (Fanny's) one day when the King (George III) and Queen (Charlotte) came to have one of their familiar chats with that gifted lady. This child, a little girl, with remarkable blue eyes and golden curls, attracted the attention of the royalties by her beauty. It may sound incredible, but it is strictly true that the subject of Fanny Burney's remark long before the close of the eighteenth century was looked upon in the forties of the nineteenth as possessed of remarkable personal attractions. Her appearance, indeed, considering her years, was extraordinary. Her exquisite features seemed untouched by time, a delicate tint of colour (perfectly natural) just flushed her cheek, and the light auburn curls, which had once been stroked by exalted hands when the American colonies were still loyal to the Crown, were long and lovely as ever. Mrs. Stratton, as she then was, may be looked on as one of those rare survivals which suggest that the years of the human frame might, under due hygienic conditions, reach an undreamed of extension. With her an absence of care, a placid mind, and a quiet interest in those around her, seem to have been the preservatives of her beauty. Of the village of Malvern she saw but little; she lived on Barnard's

Green, and like Lady Lyttelton, whose house, Peachfield, was at the foot of Malvern Common, she preferred looking at the Hills from below rather than at the view from their heights.

We may also chronicle at this point in connexion with the Hills an event historical in the growth of the Empire. Though the first authors have all passed away, the following is believed to be an accurate account of the matter.

It was in the year 1847 that three casual visitors, all three men of public reputation and high attainment, George William Lord Lyttelton, Edward Gibbon Wakefield, and John Robert Godley, were one day walking together on the top of the Malvern Hills. They were conversing on the subject of colonization, and among other things relating thereto on the complete organization practised by the ancient Greeks in sending out a new colony. In their days the parent city dispatched a carefully selected body of emigrants, representing all classes, and carrying with them the religion, laws, and social habitudes maintained in the place of origin. This highly intelligent mode of colonization, one of the fine products of the Greek brain, was contrasted with the haphazard way prevalent in this country of pouring out a stream of emigrants of all kinds, and not infrequently of the worst kinds, upon distant shores, without supplying some of the first necessities of social life, without providing free and organized government, or making provision for educational requirements, or for any religious aid, without in fact any care whether the new settlers were, or were not, to grow up into a civilized, law-abiding, and God-fearing community.

This conversation led to the question being asked, why should not an effort be made to found an English colony on some better basis, on some approach to the Greek plan of sending out a worthy representation of the old country? The idea was hailed with enthusiasm, and when it was asked where within British dominion such an experiment could be tried with a promise of success, it was Edward Gibbon Wakefield who supplied the answer. Wakefield was a remarkable man. He had long been known as an authority on colonial subjects, and had shown his administrative abilities in more than one part of Australasia. He told his two companions that in the south island of New Zealand there was a wide tract of pastoral land, eminently fitted for their purpose, with only a few hundreds of harmless Maoris, and for white occupiers none but two young

Scotch sheep-farmers, who would doubtless hand over their claims, whatever those might be, for a fair compensation.

It may be doubted whether information more promising or accurate, more timely or more fraught with future success, was ever given to a public enterprise. Wakefield spoke in the inspiring air and amid the bounteous prospect of the lofty Malverns, and it may well be that his utterance 'had taken the tone of prophecy'. At all events it was accepted then and there, and the Settlement of the Canterbury Plains, with an Association to guide and foster the project, was founded on the summit of the Malvern Hills. If any confident assurance of success, as we may easily believe, was given, that forecast was amply fulfilled. No young colony ever did better; it went from strength to strength, it rapidly enlarged the area of its production, it made the first railway ever constructed in Australasia, and showed what prosperity can be wrought by a community of free and industrious men, when untainted by class discord and unfettered by bureaucratic mistakes. It showed too the advantages of an early provision being made for religious aid and for common education. From the first there were clergy to be found zealous in their duties, and in this respect as in some others there was a sentiment of home civilization to be remarked in the province. There was too a happy admixture of classes, with intellect and culture well represented. It was in 1851 that the first band of settlers, the pioneers of the movement, 1,200 in all, sailed from the English shores, hopeful and resolute, and at this present time, sixty years after, the wide plain is set about with thriving inhabitants, while the capital alone, the city of Christchurch, with its cathedral and college, has more than 60,000 people. There has never been a greater colonial success.

In the conduct of this enterprise Lord Lyttelton took the leading part. Whatsoever may have been his exact share in the original conception, it was his hand which guided the movement and in the main ensured its completion. There were many difficulties to encounter, not a few delays and disappointments to endure, and of course some discontent for a time, but these things were manfully faced. The leading principle of the Association, that as far as its resources would allow the colonists should be provided with the primary requirements of society, was steadfastly upheld, and slowly but surely this effort to found a Church of England Settlement, with bishop and clergy, with parishes and schools, and with a wholesome and ineradicable tincture of the home life, took firm root in New Zealand. Not the least striking proof of its success was that a similar enterprise on the part of the Church of Scotland was designed and carried out in an adjacent territory of the South Island.

It was natural enough that the nomenclature given to the towns and local features of the new colony should be reminiscent of its origin. So 'Christchurch' was its capital, 'Sumner' among its earliest urban communities, while its fine port, one of the chief factors in its prosperity, was fitly christened 'Lyttelton'. A picturesque range of heights on the south horizon of the Plains was named 'The Malvern Hills', so that the generations to come might be perpetually reminded of the rock from which their fathers had been hewn.

This work of Lord Lyttelton was a great one, and will live in our colonial history. But the aim of the undertaking and the spirit by which it was animated were only the same as the aim and spirit which actuated his whole life. That life was a strenuous one, active in doing good to others in the various opportunities opened out by his position, faculties, and attainments. He used all the talents entrusted to him. Winning early distinction at Cambridge by his fine scholarship, he cultivated classical composition without ceasing, shedding off such proofs of it as (for example) his exquisite rendering into Greek verse of Tennyson's *Oenone.* His work in the cause of education was remarkable. He took an active part in the two Royal Commissions which in the middle of the last century did so much for progress, the one on the great Public Schools, the other on the Grammar (or Secondary) Schools, out of which latter sprang the statutory Endowed Schools Commission. Of the last-named he was Chairman, and did thereon, in spite of partisan opposition, a splendid work. He was also a strong supporter of improvements in female education, and led the van in the successful effort to open the University examinations to girls.

Entrusted for a long series of years with the Lord Lieutenancy of his county, he sedulously endeavoured, alike in his choice of magistrates, which was always impartial, as well as in the general administration of his office, to keep justice upright and effective. As chairman of a Board of Guardians he was constant in attendance on that thankless office, working conscientiously to keep down the mischiefs which are only too apt to creep into the details of our Poor Law. He did not possess in any marked degree that faculty for debate which is so characteristic of our statesmen, and his singularly useful career in a variety of effort proves how much may be done in public work without the adventitious aid of oratory. A higher tribute to his name was reared by his noble life, which has stamped him as one of the most eminent sons of that historical county on which the Malvern Hills look down.

These recollections all belong to a forgotten past. A strange alteration was to come. Malvern was destined, in Victoria's reign, to change from a village into a town, from high-class seclusion into middle-class villadom, from country quiet into mob resort. Those who profited by the change, and they were not a few, were naturally gratified. Those who arrived after the change, and their name was legion, thought that everything was as it always had been, and entirely in the course of nature. Only the quiet few lamented what once had been, and their lamentation did not count, for people were too busy gossiping to mind them. The operative causes of this great change were two. The first was the establishment in Malvern of the hydropathic treatment. In one point of view this was no new thing. It is probable enough that resort to the wells on the Hills for the cure of ailments had been known in the time of the monks, and had never died out altogether. We know that it was in full swing in the reign of the first Stuart, and that before the close of the next century it was revived by Dr. Wall. But the movement some seventy years later was of a different nature. The loudly advertised system of Presneitz assumed that there was a special revelation, that it superseded all ordinary medical treatment, and was applicable to all human ills. That sort of cry is the genuine voice of empiricism. The two individuals who, for purposes of personal profit, brought this beneficent system to the quiet shades of Malvern, erected an immense boarding-house for their patients, which was no doubt an advantage to many concerned, but was an eyesore to the village, and not the last which was brought about. The system took, and became a craze with crowds of people. Among those crowds were not a few to whose appearance and manners the residents and ordinary visitors were not accustomed. The social pleasantness of the place, which had been famed for generations, soon vanished. Just in proportion as the 'water cure' flourished, the higher fashion fled. Nor was there, among the perceptive, a lack of ridicule at the pretensions of the hydropathic practitioners. It was observed that when a cit, it might be an alderman, it might be a legislator, who had been eating and drinking twice as much as can be good for mortal man, and leading therewith a sedentary life, came down from London to what was then termed in the language of an auctioneer's puff 'the capital of hydropathy', ate boiled mutton and rice pudding, drank nothing but water, walked under orders up hill and down, was in bed betimes and rose early, lived in fact a sane and sanitary life, and thereupon found his liver once more active, he was proclaimed 'one of the wonders of the water-cure'. Common-sense people summed up the wonder and laughed quietly. But there were other things behind. No long time after its advent to Malvern there came to be unpleasant tales about the relations which existed between hydropathy and its lady patients. As time went on these stories grew, until they finally culminated before the public of all England in a scandalous drama, which had at first its comic scenes and moved some smiles, till it developed into a mysterious murder and a searching but futile inquest. It is not asserted that the hydropathist who was mixed up in the public mind with this tragedy was either guilty or cognizant of the crime, but his previous conduct with the lady was too patent to admit of denial, he had moved into the vicinity of the residence which she occupied with her murdered husband, and the surmises that arose were ugly. Such was the outcome of the Malvern water-cure. It damaged the place morally and socially more than its inhabitants deserved, but that was only the inevitable result, sooner or later, when that beautiful spot became the happy hunting-ground of quacks and impostors.

The other factor of the change in the condition of that Queen of the Hills, and one more operative still, was the construction of the railway. Long after the modern mode of locomotion had been established in most parts of the country, Malvern had been left dependent on the old coach traffic. There is no room for wonder that a desire for the rail arose, but it may be doubted whether the desire was met in the wisest way. It might have been possible to satisfy all reasonable requirements, and to save much outlay, while preserving some of the invaluable quietness of the older Malvern. But it is far too late to argue this point; we can only say *Dis aliter visum est.* The railway brought to Malvern a great crowd, and in some ways much prosperity, but in some others not a little deterioration. The secular solemnity of the Worcestershire Beacon has been changed by excursion trains into a bad imitation of Hampstead Heath on a Bank holiday. It is only the walks at the Wells that retain a memory of the seclusion which was once the charm and attraction of Malvern life.

But it would be distasteful not to record that the later period of Victoria's reign saw more than one valuable improvement in the condition of the Malvern Hills. Chief among them was the legislative creation of a public body charged with the conservation of the Hills themselves and of the adjacent Chase, or rather of what now remains of that wide tract of country, the relic of an historical past. There was great need for such an authority, the encroachments and invasions on the open territory having been persistent for more than 200 years. The sweeping enclosure of Welland Common in the middle of the last century did away with a picturesque and health-giving expanse, once a part of the medieval deer forest. This was only a sample, on a larger scale, of the many encroachments that went on. Happily, all such invasions, great and small, legal or illegal, are now fenced off by the jurisdiction of the Hills Preservation authority, whose work, it may be confidently hoped, will never be negligently done.

At about the same period an admirable improvement was made on the western side of the Hills. A new road, skilfully engineered, was constructed from the Wych to the Wind's Point, making a delightful drive on a high and level elevation, with a wide view over the county of Hereford to the Black Mountains in Radnorshire. Here, beyond that range, can be seen, on the rare but recurring occasions when our moist climate permits the miracle, the veil mysteriously lift, and the giant forms of Cader Idris, Plinlimmon, and other Welsh peaks loom in purple tints before the astonished eye. Those who have seen the spectacle never forget it while life endures. This road, carried out by public subscription in the teeth of some adverse criticism, is worthy of the Malvern Hills, great and lasting in its character, a worthy tribute to Nature's beauties, seldom exhibited in a scene so wide in extent and with such diversity of charm.

Our tale is told. There is no story like that of the Malverns to be found in England. It dates from immemorial antiquity, from the action of primeval and immeasurable forces ; it records millions of years of creative energy ; it traces the first footsteps of ancient man ; it is coeval with our earliest history ; it descends the stream of time with our mixed and changing fortunes, through all their vicissitudes and all their vigorous growth, till it lands us on the prosaic but, we may hope, not unproductive shores of to-day.

The Malvern Hills have lived through the whole human drama. May they still lift their heads undiminished to the sun, and still bless untold generations, born in less favoured spots, with better health and purer pleasure!

APPENDICES

I

THE LAURENTIAN HILLS IN CANADA

THE opinion of the late Dr. Holl, F.G.S., that there was a distinct correlation to be observed between the rocks of the Laurentian range and those at the southern end of the Malverns has been mentioned in 'Geologic Malvern'. This opinion is singularly corroborated by their outward appearance. The writer once looked at the distant Laurentians from a height above the Montmorency Falls near Quebec, in the clear air of Canada, and the resemblance in outline and shape to the Malverns was almost startling. It was together with a Worcestershire man, Captain Serocold, that he made the observation, which was fully assented to by his companion.

II

THE VISION OF PIERS THE PLOWMAN

By inadvertency the mention of this remarkable poem was omitted in the pages of 'Medieval Malvern'. Its author is generally supposed to have been William Langland, born in 1332 at Cleobury Mortimer in Shropshire, on the borders of Worcestershire. It will be seen from the date that he lived in a period of our history which produced striking results in our literature as well as in the social condition of the people. He was contemporary with Chaucer, and though he did not possess the genius he undoubtedly commanded the popularity of that famous writer. His verse, rough as it may have been, helped, from its wide diffusion, to fix the structure of the English language. He also, it may be remarked, lived at the time of the 'Black Death', witnessed all its horrors, the desolation which it wrought, and the social confusion which followed. He saw the accession of Richard II, and subsequently beheld his deposition. These great events seem to have influenced and coloured his poetry. His *Vision*, as he states at his opening, came to him as he was sleeping on the Malvern Hills, and the 'field full of folk' which he describes may well mean the extended view of town and country, valley and hill, spread before his eyes. It could not have been the first time on which the prospect from those breezy heights had moved the imagination of the beholder, but it was the first on which the impulse produced took the form of written poetry. A deep religious conviction runs through the whole work. His mind had been both saddened and fired by the events around him; nearly all the typical characters he introduces are meant to personify the evils and the vices of a world steeped in superstition and greed; and he ends his song with a noble exhortation to give up trust in indulgences for sin and to lead a righteous life. It is believed that his *Vision* produced as much effect on the popular mind as did the work of Wiclif, who completed his translation of the Bible in 1380. Langland, if that be his name, wrote many other poems, and died in 1400. He may certainly be claimed as the greatest writer connected with the Malverns.

III

SIR CORNELIUS VERMUYDEN

SINCE the passage relating to the disafforesting of Malvern Chase was written, the writer became aware, through careful reading of the late Mr. Gardiner's *History of the Commonwealth and Protectorate*, that Sir Cornelius Vermuyden was employed by Cromwell as his agent in a strange negotiation carried on with the Dutch States-General. Cromwell, it would seem, had already consulted with Vermuyden on an idea of his (Cromwell's) own, that England and the United Provinces might be joined together in some sort of corporate union; but this notion, as stated in a short footnote to the text of 'Stuart Malvern', came to nothing. The object of the further scheme, apparently Vermuyden's own, was that the two Governments should join in an attempt to seize upon the Spanish possessions in South America and in both the Indies, and in case of success should divide the spoil between them. The prudence of the States-General, strengthened, perhaps, by their knowledge of Cromwell's lack of financial resources, made them decline the offer. Mr. Gardiner alludes to this wild project as one of several proofs that the Protector, great in war and able in administration at home, was wholly wanting in foreign politics. But apart from this, the almost amazing fact that a man like Sir Cornelius Vermuyden, whose fortunes had been made by King Charles, should be intimately consulted and confidentially employed by Cromwell is worthy of notice.

IV

THE BATTLE OF WORCESTER

The account of the battle, and of the precedent circumstances in the city, given in the same valuable work, seems to be inaccurate in two details. It is stated that the proclamation issued by Charles, summoning the royalists to assemble on a given day at Pitchcroft, close to Worcester, was disregarded, and that in fact no such assembly took place. But Nash alludes to it and, unless we are mistaken, gives the names of some of those present on the occasion, Hornyold of Blackmore and Berkeley of Cotheridge among the number. Presence at a preliminary gathering may not prove presence at the actual fight, but we think it can hardly be doubted that some at least of the cavaliers of the county, dangerous and almost desperate as the circumstances were, responded to the call. Berkeley, certainly, was fined heavily for his share in the business, and the mortgage by means of which the fine was paid remained a burden on the estate for generations.

The other misapprehension, that the battle was fought in part on the western side of the Severn, was perhaps suggested by Mr. Frederic Harrison's essay on Cromwell in the 'Macmillan Series'. The only foundation there can be for the statement lies in the fact that there was a skirmish, for it could have been nothing more, at or near Powyke bridge, when Lambert advanced from Upton with his division, and drove the royalist force before him across the Severn bridge into Worcester. He would never have thrown his bridge of boats over the river below Diglis if there had been any chance of his rear being assailed while crossing. Not a shot, it may safely be said, was fired on the western bank of the Severn on that memorable day when Cromwell saw his fine strategy justified by the result, and his 'crowning mercy' gained.

INDEX

MALVERN DISTRICT to illustrate Military History.

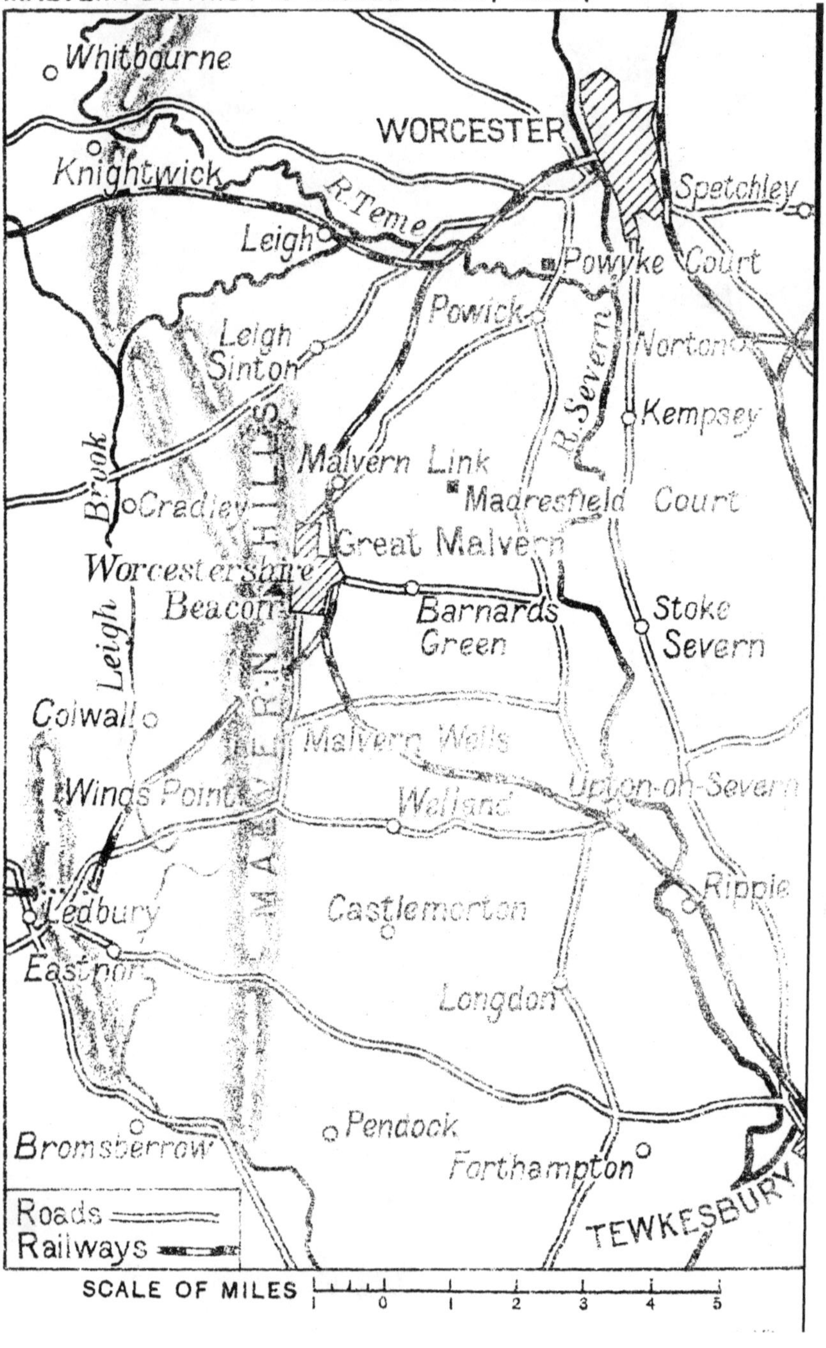

Whitbourne
WORCESTER
Knightwick
Spetchley
R. Teme
Leigh
Powyke Court
Powick
Leigh Sinton
Norton
R. Severn
Kempsey
Brook
MALVERN HILLS
Malvern Link
Cradley
Madresfield Court
Great Malvern
Worcestershire Beacon
Barnards Green
Stoke Severn
Leigh
Colwall
Malvern Wells
Upton-on-Severn
Winds Point
Welland
Ripple
Ledbury
Castlemorton
Eastnor
Longdon
Pendock
Bromsberrow
Forthampton
TEWKESBURY

Roads
Railways

SCALE OF MILES
1 0 1 2 3 4 5

CPSIA information can be obtained
at www.ICGtesting.com
Printed in the USA
BVHW031522120421
604733BV00008B/1055